Real-Time Systems Education II

Real-Time Systems Education II

June 8, 1997
Montreal, Canada

Edited by

Daniel Mossé
Department of Computer Science
University of Pittsburgh

Janusz Zalewski
Department of Electrical and Computer Engineering
University of Central Florida

Sponsored by

IEEE Computer Society
Technical Committee on Real-Time Systems (TC RTS)

Co-sponsored by

University of Pittsburgh

IEEE
COMPUTER
SOCIETY

Los Alamitos, California

Washington • Brussels • Tokyo

CENTRAL MISSOURI
STATE UNIVERSITY
Warrensburg
Missouri

IEEE Computer Society Order Number PR08256
ISBN 0-8186-8256-6
ISBN 0-8186-8258-2 (microfiche)
IEEE Order Plan Catalog Number 97TB100212
Library of Congress Number 97-76881

Additional copies may be ordered from:

IEEE Computer Society
Customer Service Center
10662 Los Vaqueros Circle
P.O. Box 3014
Los Alamitos, CA 90720-1314
Tel: + 1-714-821-8380
Fax: + 1-714-821-4641
E-mail: cs.books@computer.org

IEEE Service Center
445 Hoes Lane
P.O. Box 1331
Piscataway, NJ 08855-1331
Tel: + 1-908-981-1393
Fax: + 1-908-981-9667
mis.custserv@computer.org

IEEE Computer Society
13, Avenue de l'Aquilon
B-1200 Brussels
BELGIUM
Tel: + 32-2-770-2198
Fax: + 32-2-770-8505
euro.ofc@computer.org

IEEE Computer Society
Ooshima Building
2-19-1 Minami-Aoyama
Minato-ku, Tokyo 107
JAPAN
Tel: + 81-3-3408-3118
Fax: + 81-3-3408-3553
tokyo.ofc@computer.org

Editorial production by Penny Storms

Cover art production by Alex Torres

Printed in the United States of America by Technical Communication Services

Table of Contents

Preface

The Second IEEE Workshop on Real-Time Systems Education convened in Montreal, Canada and attracted approximately 30 participants from industry, research labs, and academia. During and after the presentations enlightening discussions took place, enriching the experience of the attendees. This collection of papers is organized, for the purpose of these Proceedings, in four categories that form separate chapters:

(1) Courses, Programs and Curricula
(2) Methods and Tools
(3) Projects and Labs
(4) Teaching Formal Methods

This categorization follows the natural approach one takes to teaching. First, the contents of a course (program, curriculum) are established and then a decision is made concerning the use of the most efficient vehicles (methods, tools, labs, etc.) to deliver the body of knowledge to the students. Formal methods were deliberately put into a separate chapter to emphasize their increasing significance in the real-time curricula. Below, a brief outline of each of the four chapters is presented.

Chapter 1, on real-time courses, programs, and curricula, comprises five papers. The first paper, by Sandén, discusses introducing design patterns to a real-time systems course. The remaining four papers present diverse approaches to particular programs in real-time systems education in Mexico (Mejia-Alvarez and Ferro), in Canada and the Unites States (Freedman and Gabrini, and Humphrey, respectively), and Taiwan (Shu and colleagues). An interesting characteristic of this batch of papers is that they outline different contexts into which real-time systems courses and curricula are introduced. They are no longer restricted to typical academic environments in computer science or engineering programs but extend to information systems programs and to cooperation with industry. The spectrum of discussed programs shows an increasing impact of real-time systems on other disciplines and environments.

Chapter 2 covers methods and tools for teaching real-time systems. Three papers on methods present different pedagogical approaches: comparing the teaching process to the engineering process (Schwarz et al.); focusing on quality issues in teaching real-time systems (Motet et al.); and basing the educational approach on the principles of problem-based learning (Nadjm-Tehrani). These are followed by two papers on tools that have been used in real-time systems education: Ghost, a tool developed in academia for scheduling analysis (Sensini et al.); and ObjecTime, an industrial tool for specification and design (Shepard et al.). The variety of approaches presented in the five papers of this chapter and their non-uniformity demonstrate the still incipient nature of methods and tools for teaching real-time systems.

Chapter 3 includes examples of laboratory exercises. Six papers present projects that vary from sound synthesis (Jacker) and satellite tracking (Barbeau), to pinball player robot (Clark) and remote car control (Mutka and Rover). The importance of networking techniques in real-time systems education, whether over a local area network or over Internet, has been demonstrated in two papers (by Hanzalek et al. and Munoz et al., respectively). As teachers of real-time systems courses can attest, having a moderately equipped lab is crucial to the success of the course. The papers comprising this chapter give an interesting overview of current developments with an inexpensive technology affordable for most educational institutions.

Chapter 4 contains four papers that investigate the impact of formal methods on the practice of engineering real-time systems in the future. Although no one can predict the outcome, there is strong feeling and consent that teaching formal techniques to real-time systems practitioners is important and beneficial. Two methods received particular attention at this workshop: the synchronous approach, discussed in the papers by Koren and Tyszberowicz, and Andre et al.; and the Petri nets approach, discussed in the papers by France and Mikojaczak. Two different perspectives for teaching both of these formal methods are presented in these papers: via integrating them with regular material within the context of a course; and via focusing exclusively on a single method in an individual course.

We would like to acknowledge the following members of the program committee for their input in the review process: Ted Baker, Sanjoy Baruah, Azer Bestavros, Alan Burns, Jorge Diaz-Herrera, Dick Eckhouse, Kevin Jaffay, Jane Liu, Nancy Mead, Al Mok, Sias Mostert, Leo Motus, Sam H. Noh, Carlos Pereira, Angelo Perkusich, Thomas Piatkowski, Ian Pyle, Raj Rajkumar, Mike Rodd, Manas Saksena, Bo Sandén, Allan Shaw, Terry Shepard, John Stankovic, Alex D. Stoyen, Lonnie Welch, Marek Zaremba.

Daniel Mossé and Janusz Zalewski
RTEW '97 Editors

Chapter 1

Real-Time Courses, Programs, and Curricula

A course in real-time software based on concurrent design patterns

Bo Sandén
Colorado Technical University
4435 N. Chestnut St.
Colorado Springs, CO 80907-3896
Email: bsanden@acm.org
http://www.isse.gmu.edu/faculty/bsanden

1. Introduction

Software design is traditionally taught by means of step-wise approaches. These are typically geared toward novices and are often too constraining for the experienced designer, who may resent the micro-management of the inherently creative design process by means of some "clerical" method. *Design patterns* allow a discussion of designs that is free from these constraints. The designer recognizes patterns in the problem and applies a design solution directly [2].

Like patterns, the *entity-life modeling (ELM)* design approach for concurrent software is a means for experienced designers to reason about designs. ELM is primarily concerned with the relationship between the software design and the problem at hand. It encourages restrictive use of concurrency where each task in the software is justified by concurrency inherent in the problem. The course discussed in this paper is based on a combination of the ELM and the pattern approaches to software design.

2. Course background and format

The course builds on a course developed at George Mason University (GMU) under a DISA grant [12, 13]. The discussion of ELM and the examples are taken from that course, and are freely available from the ASSET repository [15][1]. After the GMU course was completed, the material has been significantly improved by organizing the examples under a small number of patterns.

The course was given at GMU in a semester format with one 3-hour class meeting per week. It included a group project completed over a 4-5 week period. A course in Software Construction based on Ada [8] was a prerequisite and provided basic insight into Ada tasking. The course as presented here is given at Colo-

---

[1] The case studies mentioned in this paper are described in the html document
http://www.isse.gmu.edu/faculty/
bsanden/rtexamples.html

rado Technical University in 10 lectures over half a quarter (two 3-hour lectures per week). While this format is sufficient for the lecture material and appropriate exercises, the project is reduced to a 2-week effort, which is accomplished singly or in small groups. Unlike the situation at GMU, where each team met with the instructor for a 1-2 hour session, there is no opportunity for such meetings in the Colorado Tech format. Although two lectures on Ada tasking are included, those students with a previous course in Ada tasking have a distinct advantage.

Those who want to use the course material in a semester format may want to expand the coverage of Ada tasking and include a full team project that is started after the entire material has been covered. Remaining lecture time up to the project presentations, recapitulation and final is then used for instructor-team meetings.

3. Course structure

The course consists of the following sections:
- Introduction
- Ada tasking
- Patterns
- Periodic pattern
- State-machine pattern
- Design approaches: Entity-life modeling
- Patterns for sharing of single resources
  - Assembly-line pattern
  - Single-resource pattern
  - Comparison
- Resource-contention pattern

Each section is discussed in detail in the following. Assignments are given in conjunction with several of these sections. There is also a project component. The assignments and projects are discussed in section 5 of this paper.

3.1 Ada 95 tasking

Ada 95 is used as a teaching vehicle primarily because of the built-in tasking syntax. For this reason, the course starts with an overview of appropriate parts of

2

the Ada 95 concurrency syntax including both protected units and rendezvous. This material needs almost two class meetings and includes a few small exercises on protected units, interrupt handling, etc.

3.2 Design patterns

Object-oriented design patterns as they appear in the "gang-of-four" book [2] are introduced as a general background. The course then focuses in on concurrent patterns and in particular the periodic pattern, the state-machine pattern, the assembly-line pattern, the single-resource pattern and the resource-contention pattern. Each of these is discussed in the following. The simple periodic and state-machine patterns are presented first since they can be discussed based solely on the Ada concepts already introduced. Design approaches in general are discussed next, and finally the more elaborate patterns.

3.3 Periodic pattern

In the periodic pattern, the application must take action at specific periods. One program may manage different series of actions with different periodicity. A type problem is the throttle control in an automobile cruise control system, where a regulator task periodically compares the speed with a set target speed and adjusts the throttle.

The traditional design with a cyclic executive is discussed and contrasted to a concurrent design. An armament panel from a helicopter simulator and an avionics system [17] are used as examples. Translation of a cyclic execution scheme into periodic tasks is discussed and the basics of rate-monotonic scheduling theory are introduced.

3.4 State-machine pattern

The lecture on the state-machine pattern is prefaced by a recapitulation of the state-transition diagrams and an introduction of superstates. Examples include automobile cruise control and a power car window [8].

The state-machine pattern is used to implement software that controls a device whose behavior can be described by means of a single finite automaton [14]. It has the following structure:

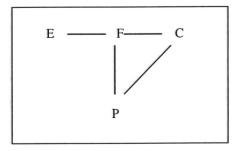

The participants in the pattern are:

E: Event captor.
F: Finite automaton (state machine).
C: One or more *activities* defined as series of periodic actions.
P: One or more input interfaces (other than E)

E captures events and sends them to F, which determines any state transition and/or actions in response to each event. *Timing events* (i.e., of the type "s seconds have passed since event x") are produced by F itself. C performs any activity relevant to the present state. P represents passive interfaces called from F and/or C.

In the implementation, E is either an interrupt handler or one or more periodic, sampler tasks. F is either a protected unit or a task. It is a task if there are timing events, which are implemented by means of delay statements. C can be represented in one of two ways. The first way is to put F and C together in one task. This amounts to incorporating the activities in the state machine itself and express them as actions triggered by timing events. The second way is to make C into one or more tasks, separate from F. In the absence of timing events, F then becomes a protected unit, which provides a means for the activity tasks to query the current state.

Examples of the state-machine pattern include:

An odometer for a bicycle where activities such as "display speed" and "display mileage" are incorporated into a task that also keeps track of the state. The state determines what is currently being displayed.

The automobile cruise control, where a regulator tasks controls the throttle and the state of cruising is represented as a protected unit [3, 8].

The automatic buoy [1, 7, 8], where activity tasks are necessary to maintain a fixed schedule of broadcasts.

3.5 Design approaches

It would perhaps seem logical to introduce the design approaches early in the course, in conjunction with patterns. Unfortunately, the design material tends to appear rather abstract to the students. For this reason, it is practical to start with the periodic and state-machine patterns as illustrations of the concrete concurrent programming constructs introduced early on.

At this stage, ELM, which is the basis of the course, is contrasted to other design approaches for real-time systems. Approaches based on (real-time) structured analysis [3, 6, 18] are briefly covered. For consistency, these approaches may be said to rely on a *transformational* pattern, where one task captures an external stimulus, then sends it to a series of other tasks, which successively transform the input into an appropriate output or other external response. Object-oriented approaches based on identifying intuitively active objects are also discussed as well as the use case approach [5]. Use cases can be employed to identify ELM threads.

3.5.1 Entity-life modeling

A complete account of ELM is provided in [16]. Aspects of the approach and particular examples are covered in [9, 10, 11]. The basis for ELM is that a real-time system must react to (or create) *events* in the problem environment, where each event is without duration but requires a finite amount of processing time. The analyst's concern is to attribute the events in a given problem to different concurrent *threads*. To do this, one creates an imaginary *trace* by laying out all events that the software has to deal with along a time line. External stimuli and actions that the software must take at specific times are included. The trace is then partitioned into *threads*. A thread is a set of events such that each event belongs to exactly one thread, and the events within each thread are separated by sufficient time for the processing of each event A set of threads that account for all the events in a problem is called a *thread model* of the problem.

As a rule, each thread maps onto a task. By basing the tasks on a thread model of the problem, we ensure that each event is handled by one task, and no task is inundated with simultaneous events. Simultaneous events are handled by different tasks. In addition to the tasks, the design contains *objects* that may or may not be shared between tasks. Something whose "life" is a thread, is referred to as an *entity*.

3.6 Patterns for single, shared resources

The patterns for single, shared resources cover the very common case where some resource user in the problem domain needs exclusive access to one shared resource at a time. (Simultaneous access to multiple resources is covered in a later section of the course; see 3.7.) The resource user may be a database operator that needs exclusive access to a record, or a part traveling along an assembly line that successively needs exclusive access to the processing stations along the line, The designer has the following choices:

> The resource users are the entities. This solution is here referred to as the *single-resource* pattern. (In the implementation, the resource users are represented by tasks and the resources by means of protected units.)

> The resources are the entities. This solution is here called the *assembly-line* pattern. (In the implementation, each resource is owned by a task that processes one request for exclusive access at a time.)

3.6.1 Assembly-line pattern

The entities in the assembly-line pattern are stations between which material or parts flow. Each station-entity operates on the part when it arrives. The diagram below shows a number of station-tasks (parallelograms) connected by protected units (trapezoids), each of which represents a queue of parts that are output by one task and input by another. The arrows indicate the direction of calls. Each call either extracts a part from the queue or inserts a part into the queue.

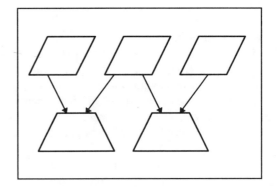

The most typical examples are physical assembly lines. In a baggage control system for an airport, for example, the stations are way-points where a piece of luggage may be routed off the main conveyor onto a baggage pick-up or loading area, or vice versa.

In a special case there is no buffering, and the stations hand over parts to each other. While the stations operate concurrently on each part, they must be synchronized pair-wise during the hand-over, which proceeds sequentially from the end backwards through the assembly line. One example of an assembly line without buffering is the LEGO car factory in [19]. This is a working toy example of a factory made from LEGO® components that makes simple cars also from LEGO components. In the implementation of an assembly line without buffering, the protected units are eliminated and the tasks are synchronized by means of rendezvous.

An interesting variation of the assembly-line pattern is represented by *data transfer* applications. Such an application receives input messages on a number of channels, transforms the messages in some fashion, and retransmits them on one or more output channels. The *order* of the messages is preserved (except for intentional re-ordering). If there are several transfor-

4

mations and several processors are available, it is desirable to set up a virtual assembly line of processors - stations. As in other assembly-line applications, each station is implemented as a task that successively transforms each incoming message. The example used in the course is a MIDI patch bay, where messages are transferred between musical instrument controllers and other electronic devices, subject to some conversion.

3.6.2 Single-resource pattern
This is the well-known pattern where a number of entities need exclusive access to one or more resources, but only one resource at a time. In contrast to the assembly-line pattern, where either the stations are physically ordered or else the order of the items passing through must be respected by the software, the single-resource pattern allows free competition for the resources, based on the priority of each entity.

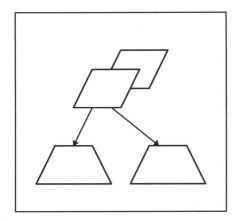

Many examples of this pattern are obvious. The point of this lecture is to illustrate cases where a simple acquire - release protocol is insufficient. The difficulty is to recognize that some non-standard problems really exhibit a single-resource pattern.

One example is the home-heating problem [4, 10] where a computer controls the heating of a group of homes. The homes share a fuel tank and due to some limitation, only 4 out of 5 homes, say, may be heated simultaneously. Each home cannot be forcibly without heat for more than, say, 10 minutes. This requires that a pool of heating "tokens" be represented. Before starting the heater, a home task must first obtain a token from the pool by calling a non-blocking *acquire* operation that returns a status parameter. If a token cannot be obtained immediately, the home tries again for up to 10 minutes. It then demands a token by calling an *insist* operation and is given a token even at the price of shutting off the heat in another home. To accomplish this, each home task periodically queries an object representing a logical on/off switch.

3.6.3 Comparison of patterns for single resources
The assembly-line and single-resource patterns are dual in the sense that a given problem can usually be implemented with either one. In the baggage-control example, there can be one task per piece of luggage (or per luggage cart) and a protected unit per station. This is not a very useful solution, however, since the pieces of luggage cannot compete for the resources but are bound by the physical arrangement of the assembly line. It also means that a new task has to be created for each piece of luggage that enters the system and destroyed when it leaves. Similarly, in the home-heating problem, one can envision an assembly line where the heating station has 4 servers for which the 5 homes must compete.

There are a number of examples where both the assembly-line and the single-resource patterns are applicable, sometimes yielding solutions with interesting differences. In the classical *remote temperature sensor (RTS)* problem first given in [20], the RTS samples the temperature of a number of furnaces and sends each temperature reading to a host computer. A single-resource solution involves one sampler tasks per furnace. The tasks contend for access to a single device for measuring the temperature and to a communication line. This is a fairly busy solution, which can be replaced by an assembly line with one thermometer task and one output task handling the sequential communication to the host. For further comparison, a solution based on the transformational pattern also exists [6].

3.7 Resource contention pattern
The resource contention pattern applies when each of a number of tasks needs simultaneous exclusive access to more than one shared resource. This is shown diagrammatically below:

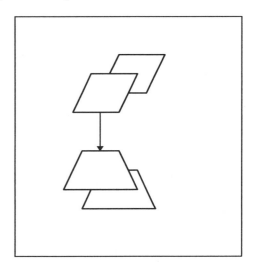

The course section on resource contention starts with a discussion of deadlock prevention. A simple graphical notation for deadlock detection is introduced. Deadlock can be prevented by making sure that there are never enough tasks to create a circular wait. In another approach, the tasks are prevented from waiting forever for a resource. If neither approach works, a static locking order or *order rule* [8] can be observed to prevent circularity. The course material elaborates on the application of order rules and cites a number of examples. The largest example, the flexible manufacturing system, is covered in the next section. Another example is an automated switchyard [8].

3.7.1 Flexible manufacturing system (FMS)

The flexible manufacturing system (FMS) is a comprehensive example of resource contention [8, 9, 11, 16]. It also illustrates other issues in ELM. For example, three different thread models are compared and shown to result in designs that differ in essential ways. The FMS also demonstrates the use of a number of Ada 95 real-time features such as protected units and types, protected procedures for interrupt handling, priority queuing and asynchronous transfer of control.

4. Course schedule

In the first offering in a 5-week format, the material was presented over 10 lectures as follows:

Lecture 1:	Introduction. Ada tasking
Lecture 2:	Ada tasking, continued. Patterns. Periodic pattern.
Lecture 3:	Finite state machines. State-machine pattern.
Lecture 4:	State-machine pattern, continued.
Lecture 5:	Design approaches: Entity-life modeling. Patterns for sharing of single resources. The assembly-line pattern.
Lecture 6:	Single-resource pattern. Comparison of patterns for managing resources.
Lecture 7:	Resource-contention pattern. Deadlock prevention.
Lecture 8:	FMS example. Automated switchyard
Lecture 9:	Project presentations
Lecture 10:	Final exam

5. Assignments, projects and exams

The course includes the following exercises:

1. A simple programming assignment on tasking and protected units. (Exercise 6.1 in [8] adapted to Ada 95.)
2. An assignment on rate monotonic scheduling.
3. A state-diagramming assignment.
4. An assignment on deadlock detection.

The term project is a design effort where the students may themselves choose the subject matter. This is usually done along the line of the examples discussed in the lectures. Projects in the first offering included: an automated parking garage, a home alarm system, an automated gas station, a beer bottling plant, a traffic light controller and the control of a network of satellites. A drawback with the short course format is that the project work starts around lecture 7, before all the material has been covered. In particular, the interesting problems with resource contention are discussed late in the course. There is no time for a student to absorb that material and come up with a project idea along the lines of the FMS.

Two open-book, open-notes exams are given: a take-home mid-term and an in-class final. Both exams consist primarily of problems of the types exercised in the assignments. In addition to the problems there are true-false questions and definition questions.

6. Conclusion

So far, the course has been given once in the Colorado Tech 5-week format. To make up for what is lost compared to the semester format used at GMU, future offerings at Colorado Tech will be more interactive. Once a design pattern has been introduced with one or more type problems, further examples will be solved on the whiteboard in cooperation with the class. This may lead to interesting developments with the class opting for an assembly-line or single-resource solution to a given problem, etc.

Another casualty of the change to a fast-paced schedule was a course summary. It is particularly useful to sum up after students present their projects, which can then be tied in with the material. In future offerings, the schedule will be rearranged to allow at least half a lecture for such recapitulation.

A final concern is the reliance on the Ada syntax, which is insufficiently covered. To compensate for this, future offerings will rely on less syntactic detail. It seems entirely possible to cover the pattern material based on a general concept of tasks and protected units without presenting very much Ada program text. Perhaps this will also make the material seem less Ada-specific and show that it is generally useful.

Acknowledgements

Most of the changes planned for future offerings are based on feedback from the students of the first offering at Colorado Tech.

The constructive comments made by the anonymous reviewers of an earlier version of this paper are gratefully acknowledged and have been applied to make the paper more consistent and readable.

References

1. G. Booch. Object-oriented development. *IEEE Transactions on Software Engineering*, 12(2):211-221, February 1986.

2. E. Gamma, R. Helm, R. Johnson, J. Vlissides. *Design Patterns: Elements of Reusable Object-Oriented Software*. Addison-Wesley, 1995.

3. H. Gomaa. *Software Design Methods for Concurrent and Real-time Systems*. Addison-Wesley, Reading, MA, 1993.

4. D. Hatley, I. A. Pirbhai. *Strategies for Real-Time System Specification*. Dorset House, 1987.

5. I. Jacobson. *Object-oriented Software Engineering*. Addison-Wesley, Reading, MA, 1992.

6. K. W. Nielsen, K. Shumate. Designing large real-time systems with Ada. *Communications of the ACM*, 30(8):695-715, August 1987. (Correction in CACM, 30(12):1073, December 1987).

7. B. I. Sandén. The case for eclectic design of real-time software. *IEEE Transactions on Software Engineering*, 15(3):360-362, March 1989.

8. B. I. Sandén. *Software Systems Construction with Examples in Ada*. Prentice-Hall, Englewood Cliffs, NJ, 1994.

9. B. I. Sandén. Designing control systems with entity-life modeling. *Journal of Systems and Software*, 28:225-237, April 1995.

10. B. I. Sandén. Using tasks to capture problem concurrency. *Ada User Journal*, 17(1):25-36, March 1996.

11. B. I. Sandén. Entity-life modeling in a distributed environment. *Proc. Fourth International Workshop on Parallel and Distributed Real-Time Systems, Honolulu, HI*, April 1996, 35 - 41.

12. B. I. Sandén. Real-time systems education at George Mason University. *Proc. Workshop on Real-Time Systems Education, Embry-Riddle Aeronautical University, Daytona Beach, FL*, April 1996, 49 - 53.

13. B. I Sandén,. A course in real-time software design based on Ada 95. *Proc., Tenth Annual ASEET Symposium, June 1996*.

14. B. I. Sandén. The state-machine pattern. *Proc. TRI-Ada, Philadelphia, PA*, December 1996, 135-142.

15 B. I. Sandén. A course in real-time software design based on Ada 95, Available through the ASSET repository as ASSET_A_825, 1996. http://www.asset.com/WSRD/abstracts/ABSTRACT_825.html

16. B. I. Sandén. Modeling concurrent software. *IEEE Software* Sep/Oct 1997.

17. D. K. Silvasi-Patchin. Real-time avionics in Ada 83. *Proc., TRI-Ada, Anaheim, CA*, Dec. 1995, 118 - 130

18. H. Simpson. The MASCOT method. *IEE/BCS Software Engineering Journal*, 1(3):103-120, 1986.

19. J.-E. Strömberg. *Styrning av LEGO-bilfabrik. Laboration i digital styrning*. Linköpings Tekniska Högskola, 1991.

20. S. J. Young. *Real-time Languages: Design and Development*, Ellis Horwood, Chichester, West Sussex, England 1982.

Real-Time Control Systems Specialization Course:
A program for the Master and Doctorate of Computer Science

Pedro Mejía-Alvarez, Bárbaro Ferro
Centro de Investigación en Computación (CIC)
Instituto Politécnico Nacional
México, DF, 07738

Abstract

There is an increasing demand for software design to support real-time control applications, such as factory automation, air-traffic control, patient monitoring systems or real-time multimedia systems. The Real-Time Control Systems Specialization track at the Center for Computing Research at The National Polytechnic Institute enable graduate software engineering students to design and develop real-time applications. Graduate students will be able to understand the design and functional timing constraints of real-time applications, such as fault tolerance, control specifications, and reliability. Also this track enable graduate software engineering students to acquire knowledge about fundamental principles of real-time computing and real-time applications, control engineering principles, and to gain experience on the design and development of real-time software. This paper describes the track motivation, the requirements and the current content of the Real-Time Control Systems course at the Center for Computing Research at The National Polytechnic Institute.

1 Introduction

The Center for Computing Research at the National Polytechnic Institute is offering a Master of Science and Phd program in the field of Computer Science. In the frame of this program a Real-Time Control Systems track is offered. The support for this Specialization Track is provided by the Real-time systems lab, the Software Technology lab, and the Automation lab [14]. The real-time specialization track provides provides several courses to show how real-time computing theory can be incorporated into control engineering and software engineering practice. In the design of this track, great attention is paid to the existance of a gap between academic courses wich expose students to real-time computing theory and practical industrial software control projects. Students who are interested in building real-time control software systems need to learn how to incorporate computing and control theory into software engineering practice.

Real-Time Control Systems Track allow the students to complete four or more full-semester, with 5 mandatory courses (80 hour-course) and 5 optional courses. This track require the study of several areas, namely, Operating Systems, Software Engineering, Control Engineering, ADA-95, and Real-Time Systems theory. As optional courses of study, we offer, Distributed systems, Simulation and Systems, Real-Time Seminar and Laboratory Practices, Intelligent Control Systems (wich covers, AI, Expert Systems, Fuzzy, and Neural Systems applied to Control Systems), Object oriented programming and Theory of Computing.

The increasing demand of applications such as trasportation control, factory automation, and comunication systems shows the importance of real-time computing. Therefore real-time computing has to incorporate control engineering and software engineering practices. In this framework, Control Engineering provides the basic principles to understand the functional behaviour of a controller, to identify the elements of a control system, and to reason about the modelling principles involved in the design and analysis of such systems.

Thus, Real-time computing theory enables the construction of control systems with timing constraints. The incorporation of software engineering practices in the design of such systems is an essential skill needed by hardware and software engineers who arquitect and build real-time systems as well as by control engineers responsible for integration, test and measurement.

Real-time course at CIC, have concentrated in computing aspects such as, operating systems and software engineering. Then, theoretical aspects of real-time computing such as resource scheduling, languages and operating system support for real-time applications. With this background some issues on control engineering are needed to support software applications and practices of a factory automation project built at the Automation laboratory.

This paper summarizes the track motivation and the most relevant features of this course and represents the collaborative efforts of several Labs at CIC to create the course.

2 Background and Rationale

2.1 Rationale

Our course provides an overview of computing issues important to the development of real-time software. We believe that software engineers need specific application domain knowledge to architect high quality real-time software systems. The main goal was to create a Real-Time Specialization Track which contains the basics of a real-time systems course followed by courses with focus on specialized topics such as, real-time software design, control engineering, simulation systems, and real-time applications.

From Fall 1996, we are offering the specialization track, and the real-time systems course.

Our goals in this track are:

- Help students to identify and understand the role of software engineers in the development of real-time software.

- Give an overview of related areas of computing, helpfull for the understanding of the real-time theory.

- Present state of the art real-time computing theory which can be applied to software engineering practice.

- Survey real-time computing issues across all phases of software development, including requirements definition, design, programming, integration, test and performance analysis.

- Bridge the gap between real-time computing theory and practical control engineering implementation.

It is important for us to motivate students to continue their study of real-time systems. In México, there are very few people doing research or teaching real-time systems. Therefore, the motivation of this course is to open this area and turn students on to *real-time computing*.

2.2 Approach

We use our experience on industrial practice for creating the Specialization Track. At Industry, engineers with knowledge in control engineering hardly understand the philosophy of software development, or some current techniques for requirements definition, design or testing. In the other side, real-time software engineers, do not have much experience or knowledge on control systems implementation.

For these reasons, we developed an integrated approach. First, we identified knowledge bases and skills needed for real-time software development, including,

- Basic computer science theory: Operating Systems, languages for real-time.

- Application domain knowledge: real-time applications requirements.

- Industrial Control Engineering practice: Introduction to control engineering, design, analysis and modeling of control systems.

- Software engineering practices: design and development techniques for real-time software systems.

Based on the structure of the CIC, we outlined a set of courses to cover the selected topics. Three Laboratories are involved in the real-time control systems Specialization Track: the Real-Time ystems Laboratory, Automation Laboratory and the Software Technology Lab. To acquaint students with actual engineering practices the automation lab provides a simulation testbed for control engineering practices.

2.3 Prerequisites

To apply for the Msc program, students must have completed a Bsc on software engineering, computer or control engineering or related areas. Priori to taking the Real-Time Control Systems Specialization Track students should have,

- Knowledge of basic computer science theory: Operating Systems, Data Bases, AI, or Control Engineering.

- Proficiency in one or more high-level programming language used to develop real-time software (e.g. C, C++, or ADA).

- Basic mathematics, such as Set Theory, Probability and Statistics, Relations.

- Some basic theory on Software Engineering.

A test is designed to enable only the best students to begin Msc studies. This test covers the basic disciplines of Computer Science and is based on the GRE test in Computer Science. Anyway, some students with enough good qualifications (based on their industrial experience) would be accepted taking an extra semester to cover basic theory on Computer Science.

To apply for the PhD program it is neccesary to have Msc in Computer Science or related areas. Also, PhD applicants must pass the test with high scores, and must provide enough evidence of industrial or academic experience. An academic committe is responsible for the admission at CIC of every PhD candidate, for this reason, an extensive evaluation of the Curricullum of every PhD candidate is performed.

3 Educational Objectives for the course

Computers control many things today. Sensors connected into computer systems that monitor real-time data and react to it. Many of the products of tomorrow will be computer controlled by real-time computer programs. Microwave ovens, automatic coffee pots, refrigerators, fuel-injected automobiles, and many other manufactured products are computer controlled by real-time programs embedded in microchips inside the product. In addition, real- time industrial control systems are becoming one of the fastest growing fields within computer science. More and more companies are automating with computer controlled real-time robots and automated machinery. Automated manufacturing is leading the advanced technology revolution as companies are ready for the competitive edge utilizing the productive, efficient, computer controlled, real-time robotic automation systems. It is crucial for today's computer science and engineering graduates to be exposed to these complex real-time programming techniques and experiment with them in a laboratory, so that they may develop the skills to write the software embedded in these sophisticated products and control systems.

Upon completion of this course students will be:

- knowledgeable in the issues of real-time systems.

- proficient in programming the techniques of real-time systems.

- competent in applying real-time programming techniques to a variety of problems.

- prepared to pursue more advanced study in real-time programming and systems.

- able to understand the literature and current research topics of real-time systems.

- knowledgeable in the software engineering issues in real-time software (task building, concurrency, interrupt handling, message passing, memory usage).

- knowledgeable in the control engineering issues, such as basic features, response characteristics and system configuration. analysis and design of control systems.

3.1 Lecture Topics

Table 1, provides a detailed list of lecture topics and assigned readings. The subsections following, contain specific educational objetives for each of set of lectures.

By studing concepts and developing real-world problems presented in the lectures and associated readings, students should be able to follow the topics presented in the following sections.

3.2 Introduction to Real-time Systems

- Determine what is and what is not a real-time system, and determine when a real-time software solution is needed when a description of an application requirement is given.

- Identify any real-time features when a description of an application is given.

- Compare and contrast real-time characteristics of some existing real-time systems.

3.3 Operating System concepts and components

- Identify main components and structures of an Operating System.

- Identify services and different mechanism for process management, storage management, I/O management, security and file management.

- Distinguish between real-time and time-sharing operating systems.

- Discuss features of real-time operating systems such as timing facilities, scheduling policies, and synchronization.

3.4 Fundamentals of Concurrency

- Describe concepts such as Process, Process scheduling, concurrency, paralellism and distributed programming.

- Descibe the phases involved in process scheduling, and the operating system interaction and structures involved.

- Describe the functional behaviour of synchronization and comunication between processes.

- Describe the fundaments problems and its associated solution related with the synchronization problem.

3.5 Fundamentals of Control Engineering

- Identify the main characteristics and concepts of a control system.

- Identify and design a computer-controlled system from a physical-control system.

- Identify and model the computation time delay effects on controlled processes.

- Describe the stability process in a control system.

Lecture Topics	Readings
Introduction to Real-time Systems.	Chapter 1,2 [2]
Operating System concepts and components	Chapter 1,3,4 [11]
Fundamentals of Concurrency	Chapter 4,5,6 [11], Chapter 7,8 key:burns 3
Fundamentals of Control Engineering	Chapter 1,2,3 [10]
Fundamentals of Real-time programming: ADA-95 Tutorial [1]	5
Real-Time Software Engineering [12]	6
Real-Time Software Design Methods [5]	7
Scheduling Issues	Chapter 13 [2]
Rate Monotonic Scheduling and Analysis	[8]
Real-Time Resource Control	Chapter 11,12 [2]
Real-Time Kernels	[4]
Hardware Issues	[9]
Reliability and Fault Tolerance	Chapter 5 [2]
Distributed Real-Time Systems	Chapter 14 [2]
Simulation of Real-Time Sistems	[13]
Project presentations	[8]

Table 1: Lecture Topics and Readings

3.6 Fundamentals of real-time programming: ADA-95 Tutorial

- Describe the differences between languages which are appropiate for real-time software development and those which are not.

- Describe the components of ADA-96, such as Ada program Units, Main programs, Ada Program Unit Lib, Lexical Units, Packages, Types, Operators, Statements, Blocks and Sobprograms, generic Units, Tasking, and Exceptions.

- Describe the concurrent programming feature of ADA-95, such as concurrent execution, the rendezvous, the select statement, the protected units, the requeue, the exceptions, the abort statement and the asynchronous transfer of control, tasking and system programming.

- Describe how is posible to program with real-time constraints using ADA-95.

3.7 Real-Time Software Engineering

- Describe the essential phases of software development.

- List and define several software life cycle models.

- Apply and analyse specification methods for real-time software development.

- Apply and analyse design methods for real-time software development.

- Analyse and discuss the ability of a chosen specification method to precisely describe the requirements and design of a given real-time system.

3.8 Real-Time Software Design Methods

- Describe, analyse and apply Real-Time Software Design Methods, such as CODARTS, and ADARTS methods.

3.9 Scheduling Issues

- Apply basic operating system concepts such as scheduling theory to software solutions for real-time problems.

- Explain the differences between static, dynamic, and best efford priority scheduling.

- Apply deterministic scheduling techniques and Rate Monotonic analysis for practical real-time applications.

- Identify the periodic and aperiodic processes and select an appropiate scheduling technique when a description of a set of jobs and their timing requirements is given.

3.10 Rate Monotonic Scheduling and Analysis

- Explain the different techinques involved in the RMA.

- Apply rate monotonic analysis to determine if a set of tasks are schedulable when timing constraints and priorities of tasks are given.

- Discuss the strengths and weaknesses of RMA.

3.11   Real-Time Resources
- Describe the concept of time, clock, process time delay, timeouts and temporal restrictions.

- Apply language support for scheduling and processes with temporal requirements.

- Describe the notion of time in terms of a programming language, using interfaces with *time* to access clocks so that the passage of time can be measured, timing requirements are represented and temporal deadlines are verified.

3.12   Real-Time Kernels
- Describe functions of a real-time kernel such as task scheduling, task dispaching, intertask communication, and memory management.

- Identify issues in the design of real-time kernels.

3.13   Hardware Issues, hardware/software interfaces, system integration, and testing
- Describe basic types of hardware used in real-time systems and characteristic performance requirements for these components.

- Discuss basic hardware/software interface issues for real-time systems.

- Describe processes for integrating real-time software with software.

- Describe the trade-offs of different hardware configurations for a given real-world application.

- List and describe laboratory equipment and devices used to develop and test real-time systems.

3.14   Reliability and Fault Tolerance
- Identify realiability, safety, and fault tolerance.

- Discuss the impact of reliability, safety and fault tolerance issues on the design of real-time software systems.

3.15   Distributed Real-Time Systems
- Explain basic concepts in the design of distributed systems such as, partitioning, allocation, communication, synchronization, concurrency control, and replication, as well as the impact of real-time system requirements on these issues.

3.16   Simulation of Real-Time Sistems
- Using the simulation control testbed, at the Automation Lab, design a real-time application to control the output of the liquid level, the temperature and pressure with timing constraints.

- Use the ADA-95 programming language for the design of such application.

4   Assignments
Several assignments and homework were designed to help students to understand the concepts presented in class lectures. Each lecture gives the student a homework to practice the concepts subject of the lecture, for which the literature for every class helps to select exercises and projects. Besides readings and homework, we included individualized projects so that students could learn more about some specialized topic. Topics chosen in the last semester (Fall 1996) are listed bellow.

- Reusability of real-time systems.

- Monitoring of real-Time Systems.

- Designing real-time distributed systems with ADA-95.

- Fault Tolerance in real-time systems.

- Tools for the design of real-time systems: Perts.

- Real-time databases.

Every topic was prepared by the student as a paper, and presented in a 2-hour lecture.

5   Application Projects
Two application projects were selected to prepare the student into the real-time contol practice.

- A good excercise and project was based on the examples provided by [8] about analysing complex real-time systems using the Rate-Monotonic Analysis. The examples provided for Message passing system and for the sonar transmission subsystem showed great support for developing analysis on practical and complex real-time systems.

- A computer controlled simulation kit at the Automation Laboratory, was given to the students with the following constraints,

Several sensors and actuators allows the simulation testbed to control the temperature and fluid level in different tanks. It consists of valves, heat switches. fluid level sensors, pressure sensors,and temperature sensors. The main pourpose of this control system is to achieve stability.

First the students must able to model the physical control system into control equations. Then, stability must be achieved doing fine tunning of the model proposed. The elements of the control system must be decomposed in concurrent activities, needed to characterize the control system. For every concurrent activity or task, real-time parameters must be identified , such as type of task (periodic, aperiodic), priority, computing time, period, and deadline.

From this characterization, an ADA-95 package must be written to perform the control, with actions such as a). Fill the tank 1 to level 40, b). heat the fluid in tank 1 to 100 degrees, c). fill tank 2 to level 40 and wait 10 seconds, d). empty tank 3, e). empty tank 3 to tanks 2 and 1, etc.

This project is still being modeled only in a PC-computer due to functional problems with the kit, but results show how students are able to model and develop timing anaylsis on a practical control system.

A Software Engineering aproach was followed for the requirement specification, design, programming and test of this project and results were presented in different reports by the students.

6 Conclusion

Students at the Ral-Time Control Specialization Track at CIC are in their second semester since the creation of the Track. Ten students are taking this track, from whom, five work at Industry. Results with the Real-Time course showed great interest in the field, and in the development of practical applications. Most of the students, previously had some background on control systems theory, which helped them to bridge the gap better between control and real-time system. As we expect, creating and teaching a course on real-time control systems for software engineers is challenging and time consuming. But courses from the Track have showed to be complementary. More details on control engineering is given in an specific course on this subject within the Specialization Track. Anyway, positive student feedback give us a reward to follow with this area, and to provide them with more of our experience in three exciting fields of computing science, Software Engineering, Control and Real-Time Systems.

References

[1] J.Barnes, "Programming in ADA-95", *Addison Wesley, Reading MA*, 1995.

[2] A.Burns and A. Wellings, "Real-Time Systems and Programming Languages", *Addison Wesley, Second Edition*, 1997.

[3] G. Booch, "Object oriented analysis and design with applications", *Benjamin Cummings, Redwood City, CA*, 1994.

[4] K.Ghosh et-al, "A Survey of Real-Time Operating Systems", *Technical Report GIT-CC-93/18, College of Computing, Georgia Institute of Technology,Atlanta, Georgia*, 1994.

[5] H.Gomma, "Software Design Methods for Concurrent and Real-Time Systems", *Addison Wesley, Reading, MA*, 1993.

[6] M.Gonzalez Harbour et al, "Course Notes, Real-Time Systems Programming:Impact of the new ADA-95 and POSIX standards", *XI Laredo Summer Courses, Universidad de Cantabria, SPAIN*, 1995.

[7] C.L.Hoover, "The Role of Software Engineering in Real-Time Software Development: An Introductory Course", *Proc. 8th. SEI Conf. Software Engineering Education*, R.L.Ibrahim, Springer Verlag, Berlin 1995, pp-167-186.

[8] M.Klein et-al, "A Practitioner's Handbook for Real-Time Analysis: Guide to Rate Monotonic Analysis", *Kluwer Academic Publishers, Boston, MA*, 1993.

[9] P.A.Laplante, "Real-Time Systems Design and Analysis: An Engineer's Handbook", *IEEE Press, Psicataway, NJ*, 1993.

[10] N.S.Nise, "Control Systems Engineering, Second Edition", *Addison Wesley, Reading, MA*, 1995.

[11] A.Silbershatz, P.B.Galvin, "Operating System Concepts, Fourth Edition", *Addison Wesley, Reading, MA*, 1995.

[12] I.Somerville, "Software Engineering, 5th. Edition", *Addison Wesley, Reading, MA*, 1996.

[13] M.F.Storch, "A Framework for the Simulation of Complex Real-Time Systems", *PhD. Thesis, Technical Repor UIUCDCS-R-96-1983, University of Illinois at Urbana Champaign*, 1996.

[14] P.Mejia and B.Ferro, "Towards the Creation of the CIC's Real-Time Systems Laboratory", *Real-Time Systems Education, IEEE Computer Society Press, Los Alamitos CA*, 1996.

[15] J.Zalewski, "Real-Time Systems Education", *IEEE Computer Society Press, Los Alamitos CA*, 1996.

Cooperation with Industry in Real-time Systems at CRIM

Paul Freedman, Lead Researcher, Software Development Tools and Methods
Philippe Gabrini, Vice-President, R&D Management
Centre de recherche informatique de Montréal

Abstract

Given the increasing pressures on the private sector to be competitive in the world market-place, governments, industry, and universities have come to understand the importance of encouraging technology development within the framework of technology transfer. The Computer (science) Research Institute of Montreal (CRIM) or in French, le Centre de recherche informatique de Montreal, was created in 1985 to address such needs by pooling resources from the public, private, and para-public sectors in the province of Québec to perform R&D activities in key areas of information technologies including real-time systems.

In this article, we begin by presenting CRIM, its mission and activities, and then we describe the kinds of education and technology transfer which take place at CRIM with specific emphasis on two collaborative projects involving industrial partners, CRIM staff, university professors and their graduate students in the area of computerized control systems.

1   CRIM at a glance

Traditional university-industry cooperation works well when there are few players involved, such as a single professor or perhaps a small team of professors (and their graduate students) at the same university collaborating with a single company. Indeed, most universities have created industrial liaison centers to help university professors prepare research contracts, define and administer intellectual property policy, commercialize their research and establish contacts with potential industrial sponsors. But when there are many players involved such as several companies, different research organizations and several professors from different universities, the administrative and technical aspects of defining a single project with multiple goals, and of keeping the ball rolling, requires much more than the scientific expertise that university professors can provide.

For this reason and in response to a university-led initiative, the Computer (science) Research Institute of Montreal (CRIM) was created by the Québec government in 1985 as a private, non-profit corporation. CRIM's base funding is provided by the provincial Ministry of Industry, Commerce, Science and Technology (MICST) and supports the infrastructure necessary to initiate and conduct R&D projects. CRIM is managed by a Board of Directors with 16 members: 7 university representatives (mostly Vice-Rectors), 7 industrial representatives, 1 representative from the provincial government, and CRIM's President and CEO.

As of this writing, CRIM has a total of 92 members, including 75 companies active in various information technologies, and 10 universities in Québec.

Today, CRIM's mandate is defined in terms of four broad interconnected goals:

- To implement pre-competitive and industrial R&D projects in key areas of specific interest to CRIM members, fostering synergy between the finest resources in CRIM, universities, corporations and related organizations;

- To transfer knowledge by developing tools and activities for the purposes of training, dissemination, technology transfer and monitoring, all of which allow advanced research findings to be converted into innovative solutions accessible to users, thereby helping them increase their competitive position and their ability to contribute to economic development;

- To contribute to the training of a highly skilled work-force, particularly at the graduate level, by involving students from universities across Québec in R&D projects, and by actively supporting the development of university programs in information technology;

- To lead in promoting linkages between corporations, universities and other organizations interested in the latest developments in information technology.

Over the years, CRIM has established four *divisions*, dedicated to offering to its members supplementary services which complement its R&D activities. Contrary to the R&D groups or *units* (to be described in the next section), the divisions must be financially self supporting. For example, the "Applied Software Engineering Center" (ASEC) was created in 1991; its mission is to assume a leadership role with regards to technology transfer in software engineering. ASEC is an affiliate academic member of Carnegie-Mellon University's Software Engineering Institute (SEI) and acts as the SEI clearinghouse in Canada and in the French speaking world. ASEC's main objectives are to help companies improve their own level of software engineering maturity, and to provide training in software engineering techniques.

Early in 1997, CRIM was subject to careful review by the provincial government which made evident its measure of success. Over the past five years, CRIM has undertaken 144 R&D projects, most of them now completed. Among these, 106 were industrial and 38 pre-competitive, and a total of 287 graduate students were involved. Currently, there are 33 active projects involving 65 students. Today, CRIM has more than 130 regular employees, an annual budget of over 16 million dollars and a level of self financing of 72

Except for the divisions, the majority of CRIM's staff is directly engaged in R&D activities and hold either a Master's degree or a doctorate in areas as diverse as computer science, engineering (electrical, computer, etc.), science (physics, mathematics, etc.), or psychology. This makes it possible for CRIM to bring an interdisciplinary expertise to the various projects it undertakes.

While CRIM continues to be a Québec-based organization, it has much more than a provincial focus. Some of its industrial members, for example, have headquarters outside of Québec, and CRIM itself is also a member of various national organizations. In addition, CRIM has established international relationships with several research organizations including the Massachusetts Institute of Technology (MIT) and the Software Engineering Institute (SEI) at Carnegie-Mellon University and the Software Engineering Laboratory at the University of Maryland in the United States, INRIA and LAAS/CNRS in France, GMD and Forwiss in Germany. Such relationships make it possible, for example, for students involved in CRIM projects to conduct part of their research elsewhere.

In the next section, we'll turn to an examination of R&D at CRIM. As can be expected, there is some interaction between the R&D units and the divisions, even though they have different objectives.

2 R&D at CRIM

As noted earlier, large R&D projects involving many players from industry, university and other research organizations, demand professional, scientific and administrative management. CRIM has responded to this challenge by organizing its R&D units under a dual leadership: a Lead Researcher on the scientific side, and a Project Director on the management side. In this manner, the scientific and administrative aspects of proposal definition as well as of the actual project can both be managed by the people who can do them best. This is a distinct advantage over university research, where the professor in charge is obliged to assume the responsibility of project management.

Typically, Lead Researchers have cross appointments as Adjunct Professors in computer science or electrical engineering departments at one of the four universities in Montreal. In this way, they are able to foster and maintain close ties with university colleagues and co-supervise graduate students, both at CRIM and at the university. On the other hand, Project Directors all have extensive project management experience in industry and are in a good position to make sure that projects go ahead as scheduled, that budgets are met and that deliverables are produced on time.

Given the accelerated pace of technology development, what constitutes leading edge research today can quickly become industrial expertise tomorrow. For this reason, CRIM is careful to track the shifting technology transfer window by abandoning activities to the private sector and starting new ones in emerging areas. Just now, there are five R&D units:

- Software Development Tools and Methods;

- Human-Computer Interaction;

- Knowledge-Based Systems;

- Telecommunications and Distributed Systems;

- Information Highway Applications.

Expertise in real-time systems can be found in the first unit, Software Development Tools and Methods, which is active in the following areas:

- object-oriented software development methodologies and CASE tool support;

- software and reference architectures;

- standards and processes in software development;

- programs for the measurement of process quality and software products;

- methods and tools for process modeling and improvement;

- real-time embedded control systems, including robotics.

As a service to the community at large, free, half-day seminars on software engineering, embedded systems, robotics are offered in conjunction with CRIM's Training division. Such seminars are designed to communicate some of the flavour of current technology and problems on the horizon. In addition, free presentations by renowned local, national and international invited speakers are offered regularly, covering theoretical, technical and methodological aspects of software engineering.

But cooperation with industry in the best sense takes place elsewhere, within the context of R&D projects bringing together industrial partners, CRIM staff, university professors and their graduate students. In the next two sections, we shall more carefully explore this topic by reviewing two inter-locking projects.

3 Train informatisé

In order to cope with the growing complexity of computerized systems in general, new products have appeared, especially in the field of telecommunications, to assist in software development by making it possible to model and thereby analyze requirements; some products provide, in addition, facilities to partially automate the generation of the target executable for a target host (which is typically different from the development host).

In conjunction with Bombardier's Transportation Equipment Group (St.Bruno, Québec), CRIM began a two year project in January 1995 called "Train informatisé" (in English, "Computerized Train") to evaluate these new methods and tools for the software development of computerized train systems characterized by behavior which is both time-driven or scheduled, associated with closed loop control, and event-driven or reactive, associated with detecting alarms, responding to infrequent operator input, etc. As a result, respecting timing requirements must be considered as an extension to logical correctness instead of as a measure of performance, as is typically the case in telecommunications [Freedman et al. 1996b].

Upon completion of a survey of the state-of-the-art in software development techniques, methods and tools for real-time systems [Freedman et al. 1995], we chose "ROOM" (Real- Time Object-Oriented Modeling) [Selig et al. 1994] and its CASE tool "ObjecTime" for further study. In particular, ROOM/ObjecTime makes it possible to design reactive systems in terms of communicating objects called actors, whose behaviors are defined by finite state machines which exchange messages over dedicated point-to-point links.

In order to better understand the ROOM/ObjecTime approach and better evaluate the merits of automated software development for new generation train systems, we created a test- bed (PC compatible computer hosting the LynxOS real-time operating system, connected to a Sun workstation via Ethernet). A simplified model of Bombardier's new generation train tilting system [Lanoix 1995] was then used as the starting point for our experiments. Note that this model has both scheduled and reactive behaviors: performing periodic closed-loop tilting sensing and control, and detecting loss of messages in the interactor communication. Careful attention was paid to the way in which an executable incorporating the ObjecTime ÒMicro Run-Time SystemÓ for our testbed (target platform) could be generated directly and automatically from the model. Key elements here are the grouping of co-operating actors into independent threads of concurrency, and the respect of periodic timing constraints at runtime. While much of the work remains confidential, CRIM presented preliminary results at the IEEE Real-Time Technologies and Applications Symposium last year [Gaudreau and Freedman 1996].

At the end of the project, the key CRIM researcher was hired by Bombardier's Transportation Group. While this can be seen as having a negative impact on CRIM (loss of expertise, loss of continuity, etc.), such departures do contribute in a very mundane but important way to the technology transfer part of CRIM's mission. This is of great importance to industry and personnel turnover is a fact of life at CRIM.

Note that in addition to the ROOM/ObjecTime focus, the same ÒTrain InformatiséÓ also included 'transfer' objectives addressed by CRIM's ASEC division related to software pro- cess improvement. In particular, ASEC staff were called upon to review and compare emerging standards related to software engineering (IEEE, SEI's CMM, ISO-9000) to help Bombardier staff formulate better guidelines for controlling the quality of software sub-contracting, i.e. the quality of computer-based subsystems developed under contract by their suppliers.

In many ways, the "Train informatisé" project is typical of the projects called *industrial research* at CRIM:

- the project was designed to address multiple objectives, combining transfer elements with technology evaluation (here, a CASE tool designed for the object-oriented software development of real-time systems) in a 'real-world' setting;

- the industrial partner is the project sponsor and as a result, any new intellectual property is typically owned by the industrial partner;

- project planning is defined in terms of precise deliverables (reports summarizing key findings);

- CRIM professional staff, not graduate students, are responsible for conducting the necessary work in collaboration with the industrial partner;

- although the contractual nature of the collaboration makes the research results confidential, the ideas (but not the details) become the subject of publications;

- at the end of the project, a special kind of Òtechnology transferÓ sometimes takes place when staff leave CRIM to become employees of the industrial partner.

As we shall see in the next section, CRIM was able to successfully leverage "Train informatisé" by developing a sister project called "Modélisation et analyse formelle de logiciels de contrôle-commande" (in English, "Formal modelling and analysis of computerized control software") or "LOCO" for short, with more research-oriented goals.

4 LOCO

LOCO is a two year research project which began in January 1996 with the mandate to address more exploratory elements of the ÒTrain informatiséÓ project, in collaboration with Michel Barbeau, Professor in the Department of Mathematics and Computer Science at the University of Sherbrooke (Sherbrooke, Québec) and more recently, Manas Saksena, Professor in the Department of Computer Science at Concordia University (Montréal, Québec). The project is jointly funded by Bombardier's Transportation Equipment Group and the Natural Sciences and Engineering Research Council of Canada (NSERC). In particular, most of this shared industry-government funding is destined for graduate student support at both the University of Sherbrooke (under the direction of Barbeau) and at CRIM (under the shared direction of Freedman and Saksena).

Of particular interest in the LOCO project is the modelling and analysis of the kinds of temporal requirements typically associated with real-time computerized control systems and how they may be addressed by object-oriented software development methods. In particular, our work with ROOM/ObjecTime in "Train informatisé" provided the technological context for the LOCO project, which also combines elements of our previous collaborative research with the researcher Daniel Simon at INRIA-Sophia Antipolis in the area of computing architectures for robotic systems e.g. [Simon et al. 1997].

Work at CRIM thus far has concentrated on characterizing typical temporal requirements [Freedman et al. 1996a] and on the evaluation of the Rate Monotonic Analysis framework which makes possible certain kinds of schedulability analysis at design time. Our goal is to develop ways of defining ROOM models in order to perform such rate monotonic analyses and to study the suitability of current ROOM semantics for expressing temporal requirements. More recently, we are developing guidelines for ROOM modelling and for the implementation of the ObjecTime Micro Run-Time System in order to promote schedulability analysis and more deterministic runtime behavior [Saksena et al. 1997].

The LOCO project is typical of what is called *pre-competitive research* at CRIM:

- the project focus is on studying problems in relation to a 'real-world' setting, and on developing new ideas, building research prototypes, etc.;

- project objectives are subject to careful planning, but not the research work per se;

- the project is co-sponsored by the industrial partner and a governmental funding agency (grant program) and as a result, ownership of new intellectual property is vested in CRIM and its university partners by the governmental funding agency;

- university professors are involved, along with their graduate students, who typically work alongside CRIM employees (and whose thesis work is co-supervised by CRIM researchers);

- research results are subject to publication;

- at the end of the project, a different kind of 'technology transfer' sometimes takes place when the graduate students involved become CRIM employees. In this sense, CRIM can be seen as a sort of stepping stone on the way from academia to industry. By taking part in CRIM's R&D projects, students gain valuable experience by being exposed to the constraints of industrial development as well as to the depth of academic research. This shows that there is a definite advantage for the future careers of the students being involved in university-industry projects, and represents added value when compared to traditional (academic) training.

Indeed, we note that the key staff person who left CRIM to work for our industrial partner at the end of the "Train informatisé" project had himself come to CRIM just one year earlier as soon as he completed his masterOs degree at one of the universities in Québec. Moreover, his graduate work was conducted within the context of yet another pre-competitive research project at CRIM for which he received financial support. In this sense, his university -¿ CRIM -¿ industry trajectory illustrates just how CRIM can serve as useful 'stepping stone" with value added along the way.

5 Conclusions and lessons learned

An analysis of CRIM's history over the last ten years makes it possible to identify key elements of its measure of success. We now present the most important in the spirit of "lessons learned".

- CRIM places a special emphasis on collaborative research: developing partnerships linking universities, the private sector, governmental agencies, and the greater research community. In particular, our independent status makes it possible for CRIM to present itself as 'neutral territory' when bringing together professors from multiple universities to work together within a common project.

- CRIM projects are developed to respond to industrial needs and in this sense, CRIM has no particular research agenda to 'sell' to industrial sponsors. Rather, projects are built upon established expertise which continues to evolve at CRIM as a function of project requirements (within the confines of our R&D groups).

- CRIM projects invariably address multiple goals, combining short-term transfer elements with medium-term exploratory R&D elements.

- CRIM members collectively ensure that CRIM tracks the shifting technology transfer window by abandoning activities to the private sector and starting new ones in emerging areas.

- CRIM has both scientific and managerial infrastructures for developing, conducting, and coordinating R&D activities. In this way, CRIM staff 'keep the ball rolling' and work to ensure that all parties are kept informed and committed to the project objectives. (This is especially difficult to do in a university setting.)

In addition, collaborative projects at CRIM with industry help:

- promote university interest in areas judged important by the industrial community, i.e. in areas which become the subject of collaborative work with industry at CRIM;

- create new funds for graduate student support (for a total of 5 students in the LOCO project), for their computing resources, for their travel to conferences, etc.;

- enrich the graduate student experience, by embedding graduate student research within the context of collaborative projects so that the work performed counts towards the project and an advanced degree. Of course, such embedding poses its own challenges, since the student is sometimes subject to conflicting advice and direction from the university professor (thesis advisor) and the researcher at CRIM (thesis co-advisor). But since such conflict is part of the everyday work environment, it in itself contributes to the enrichment!

6 References

[Freedman et al. 1996b] P. Freedman, D. Gaudreau, R. Boutaba, A. Mehaoua. "Two Real-Time Solitudes: computerized control and telecommunications", IEEE Real-Time Applications Workshop, Montréal, Québec, October 22-24, 1996.

[Freedman et al. 1996a] P. Freedman, M. Litoiu, M. Bari. "Characterizing the temporal requirements of embedded control systems", Technical Report CRIM-96/08-61, août 1996.

[Freedman et al. 1995] P. Freedman, J.-M. Goutal, Y. Leborgne, D. Gaudreau. "Étude sur des techniques, méthodes et outils de développement logiciel de systèmes temps-réel", Technical report CRIM-95/12-40, décembre 1995.

[Gaudreau and Freedman 1996] D. Gaudreau, P. Freedman, "Temporal Analysis and Object-Oriented Real-Time Software Development: a Case Study with ROOM/ObjecTime", IEEE Real-Time Technologies and Applications Symposium, Boston, Massachusetts, June 10-12, 1996.

[Lanoix 1995] Daniel Lanoix, "Bombardier's new generation tilting system", *IEEE Canadian Review*, summer 1995.

[Saksena et al. 1997] M. Saksena, P. Freedman, P. Rodziewicz, "Guidelines fo the Automated Implementation of Executable Object Oriented Models for Real-Time Embedded Control Systems", submission to IEEE RTSS '97.

[Selic et al. 1994] B. Selic, G. Gullekson, P. Ward, Real-Time Object-Oriented Modeling, Wiley, 1994.

[Simon et al. 1997] D. Simon, P. Freedman, E. Castillo, "Design and Analysis of Synchronisation for Real-Time Closed Loop Control in Robotics", *IEEE Transactions on Control Systems Technology*, 1997, to appear.

Teaching Real-Time Systems in an Information Systems Program

Lih-Chyun Shu, Shyue-Horng Shiau, Huey-Min Sun, Chang-Ming Tsai, and Tei-Wei Kuo[†]

Dept of Information Management   [†]*Dept of Computer Science and Information Engineering*

Chang Jung University   *National Chung Cheng University*

Tainan, Taiwan 711, R.O.C.   *NatiChiayi, Taiwan 621, R.O.C.*

shulc@mail.cju.edu.tw   *ktw@cs.ccu.edu.tw*

Abstract

Computers have entered into all walks of our life and products made by real-time technology are innumerable. Higher education institutions must see this trend and prepare their gradates to satisfy society's needs. Information Systems curriculum recommended by DPMA [1] is not adequate in this regard. In this paper, we explain our rationale in incorporating real-time systems into our information systems program, the course contents, laboratory setup, projects given to students, and experiences we gained in teaching this course.

1 Introduction

As computers become smaller, faster, cheaper and more reliable so their range of application widens. Today not only more and more real-time systems (RTS) are being built, they are becoming indispensable in our daily life. In fact, real-time systems has been termed a generic enabling technology for many important application areas including: multimedia, virtual reality, program trading, process control, air traffic control, space applications, to name just a few[13].

Information systems (IS) operate by transforming input data into useful information. Although a large proportion of all IS programs are business-oriented, we lean toward a broader perspective that IS development applies to all problem domains from the traditional area of business to education to science to engineering.

Like RTS, IS require their output information to be both correct and timely. All IS have response time requirements, usually in the loose form of "as fast as possible". When an IS is associated with clearly specified timing constraints, it becomes real time. It is the correctness and timeliness requirements that have made the development of RTS much more challenging than other IS. Today, many IS used in business, called management information systems (MIS), are moving from batch processing and time sharing to the domain of RTS due to technology advances and managers' increasing information demands [13, 8].

Compared with computer science graduates, IS students are weaker in mastery of paradigms from mathematical, scientific, and engineering disciplines such as theory, abstraction, and design. Managers have been complaining about the college preparation of entry-level personnel, saying IS graduates lack the technical foundation to assimilate rapid technological change. It has been recognized the IS model curriculum recommended by DPMA [1] is not appropriate in this regard[4]. It is our intention to include the study of real-time and other related disciplines to prepare our students with solid foundation so that they can go beyond the superficial and specialize over a spectrum from information systems to computer and software engineering. In this paper, we introduce our IS program and explain why and how we incorporate RTS into our curriculum. We then describe the course contents, laboratory setup, projects given to students, and experiences we gained in teaching this course.

2 Curriculum Development

Our IS program is divided into three knowledge units: information management, mathematical and computing sciences, and management science. The first two units emphasize the in-

This work was partially supported by the National Science Council under grant NSC 86-2213-E-309-001.

19

creasingly greater complex problem-solving skills demanded of the contemporary information system developer. Together with the third unit, they prepare our graduates for the challenge of developing large complex integrated systems and of capitalizing on rapid advances in technology.

It is worth noting that our decision to emphasize mathematical and computing core courses was influenced by the comment made by DPMA: "As IS becomes more quantitative and develops additional analytical methods, the IS professional must develop sufficient understanding of the relevant software and hardware engineering principles." [1] Unfortunately, DPMA model curriculum does not satisfy this need. Because current trend in building RTS involves paradigms from mathematical, scientific, and engineering disciplines [14], it is our feeling that incorporating RTS into our curriculum can further enhance our students' analytical capability. This course is part of a series of system courses we offer, e.g., distributed and networking systems, functional systems in business, etc.

Based on our course material, we require the prerequisites for our RTS course to be operating systems, system analysis, and data structures. Because these courses are taught at sophomore and junior levels, we decide to offer RTS as an elective at the senior level with 3 credits.

3 Course Contents

In designing our course contents, the survey results compiled by Zalewski [17] are of valuable help. The course syllabus suggested in [18] outlines a four-layer paradigm for teaching RTS. This paradigm is best suited for computer science or engineering students. Because our program's emphasis in both computing and management sciences, we must tailor the paradigm to our needs. In particular, we place less emphasis on hardware architectures, but more emphasis on software architectures applicable to the construction of both information systems including management information systems and real-time systems. This consideration also leads us to the decision that we prepare our course notes, instead of using a textbook.

Our course is composed of the following units: (1) introduction, (2) classification of RTS, (3) typical examples, (4) real-time system architectures, (5) real-time programming languages, in particular Ada, (6) real-time operating systems and databases, and (7) implementation projects.

To motivate our students, we used a real-time example from program trading [15]. Program trading is a computerized trading strategy in which investors profit from the difference in price betweens a group of stocks and stock-index futures on those same stocks. Stocks are sold and futures are purchased, when the sum of the stock prices exceeds that of the futures; stocks are bought and futures are sold, when futures price rises above that of the stocks. In this kind of trading, speed is essential to take advantage of the price discrepancy. Each trade order is associated with a clearly specified response time requirement, which some people call it firm deadline [5]. If the order can't be done before the deadline, it is aborted to avoid money loss. Because our students have taken mangement-related courses, the terminologies used in program trading are familiar to them and they can quickly pick up the essence of the example. More importantly, students realize there are computerized systems whose correctness depends not only on logical correctness but also on the timeliness of output.

To teach students RTS specification, design and development, we used the RTS architecture proposed in [8]. Using this framework serves two purposes. Because it is developed from Zachman's architecture for IS [16] which depicts all aspects of IS architecture from high-level business strategies to system coding, students have a clear picture of structuring the development of IS. Like IS, RTS are increasingly complex and difficult to build and maintain. The RTS architecture described in [8] provides solutions to critical RTS concerns such as timing, predictability and deadlock. It also categorize various specification and design techniques used in RTS. Through the framework, students understand that each technique has strengths and weakness, and therefore who in the development cycle would best utilize each tool or methodology.

To transform top-level requirement specifications into executing machine code requires a programming language. We present to students 3 classed of programming languages used in building RTS, i.e., assembly languages, high-level sequential languages and concurrent languages. These languages' uses in RTS have historic reasons. Students must understand the weakness of assembly and sequential programming languages used in building RTS. We discussed the desirable features of real-time concurrent languages such as security, reliability, flexibility, simplicity, portability, and efficiency [3]. These criteria are taken into consideration when we choose Ada as our focused language in the class.

Real-time databases is a relatively new research area, but is becoming increasingly important. Data are essential resources in RTS; maintaining data consistency while still satisfying timing constraints is a practical but challenging problem. The first author of this paper has done some research in this area [9, 7, 12, 11, 10], we devoted some time in discussing this interesting topic.

4 Real-Time Systems Laboratory

Over the years, we have set up a minimally equipped RTS laboratory with a Sun SPARCstation and several Pentium PCs. The Sun workstation has two SuperSPARC 20 CPUs and runs under Solaris 2.5.1. Solaris provides many crucial features for real-time applications such as fixed priority real-time process, high resolution timers, preemptive scheduling, deterministic and guaranteed dispatch latency, process priority inheritance. We installed Gnat Ada compiler in Solaris for students to do programming projects. One of our PCs runs under LynxOS 2.4. Because Solaris and LynxOS have different characteristics, we teach students how these differences will affect our decision in picking a real-time operating systems. For example, Solaris provides a higher resolution timer than LynxOS, hence is suitable for a lot more applications.

Real-time systems often need to interface with many I/O devices, e.g., sensors, displays, timers, etc. We have some character LCD (Liquid Crystal Display) modules donated by vendors. We require students use the software modules described in [6] to experiment things like displaying bar graphs, defining symbols based on a 5x7 dot matrix, displaying ASCII strings, etc. As a result, students' background in manipulating peripheral operations is strengthened.

5 Implementation Projects

In order for students to gain practical experiences, implementation projects are indispensable. We describe the projects themselves in this section and experiences we learned in the next section. In the first project, we require students to use Ada tasking to simulate the client-server structure in elevator's operation. On every of the one hundred floors in a skyscraper, people request for elevator services. The elevator receives and processes requests in the following manner: it continues servicing in one direction (up or down) until there is no more request ahead in that direction. By then, it changes the direction and continues its services. The elevator is assumed to be on the first floor initially. They model each client's requests in the nth floor in the following way:

```
loop
   generate a request
   wait for the request to be serviced
   sleep for random seconds
end loop
```

For each client, they should print out arrival and destination information. The server task processes request in an FIFO order and must print out servicing information, e.g., "pick up a guest on the nth floor going for the mth floor", "a guest leaves on the mth floor" etc.

Our second project is to simulate arbitrage trading [2], a firm real-time example. Two input data streams send in gold prices from London and New York gold markets, respectively. Currency exchange rates come in from another data stream. Students are required to program writer and reader tasks. The writer task randomly changes gold prices and currency exchange rates. and writes the data into a ring buffer. The reader task reads the data from the ring buffer, calculates the price difference, and displays the results on the screen. The calculation must be done before the writer task writing a new data, otherwise the dispay job will be aborted.

6 Teaching Experiences

To improve teaching quality, it is important to select proper examples and projects, taking students' background into consideration. Our decision to use a few business-oriented cases for both instruction and implementation purposes has motivated students quite a bit. However, pedagogic examples are still lacking, especially in information systems domain.

A course with plentiful teaching materials like RTS is best taught in two consecutive semesters — first semester on theories and principles and second semester on implementation. Collaborative teaching will especially be useful where academic folks focus on well-established paradigms and industry folks can infuse knowledge in industrial practice into the course. More importantly, industry folkes can keep us informed about newest technology transfer and problems encountered.

After students implemented the elevator project, we gave them hints about making it a true real-time project. For example, each client task can be made to become truly periodic by using Ada 95's "delay until" statement. The server task can have an "admission control" module to provide timing guarantees to admitted clients. This kind of service may not be applicable to the elevator case, but is the case in many multimedia servers. Instead of telling students the multimedia example directly, this stepwise instruction technique gave students a chance to think more independently.

7 Conclusion

Real-time computing is becoming a critical enabling technology for many important applications not only in many industrial sectors but also in the business world. It is also becoming an essential discipline in the field of computer science and engineering. We feel that it will soon become an important knowledge unit in information systems programs. Because the demand for college graduates with solid background in real-time technology is increasing rapidly, this kind of environmental force will trigger and shape curriculum reassessment in many academic institutions. We have taken a small step in this direction and still have a long way to go in our pursuit of curriculum excellence.

References

[1] DPMA, Information Systems: The DPMA model curriculum for a four year undergraduate degree. Data Processing Management Association, 1990.

[2] R. Abbott and H. Garcia-Molina. Scheduling real-time transactions: a performance evaluation. In *Proc. 14th Intl Conf on Very Large Data Bases*, pages 1–12, August 1988.

[3] A. Burns and A. Wellings. *Real-Time Systems and Their Programming Languages*. Addison Wesley Publishing Company, Reading, Mass., 2 edition, 1996.

[4] T. Fabbri and R. A. Mann. A critical analysis of the ACM and DPMA curriculum models. *Journal of Computer Information Systems*, pages 77–80, Fall 1993.

[5] J. R. Haritsa, M. J. Carey, and M. Livny. On being optimistic about real-time constraints. In *9th ACM SIGACT-SIGMOD-SIGART Symposisum on Principle of Database Systems*, pages 331–343, April 1990.

[6] J. J. Labrosse. *Embedded Systems Building Blocks*. R&D Publishers, Lawrence, Kansas, 1995.

[7] M.-C. Liang, T.-W. Kuo, and L. Shu. A class of abort-oriented protocols based on the notion of compatibility. In *Proc. of the 3rd international workshop on real-time computing systems and applications*, Oct. 1996.

[8] D. Schoch and P. Laplante. A real-time systems context for the framework for information systems architecture. *IBM Systems Journal*, pages 20–38, 1995.

[9] L. Shu. Abort-oriented concurrency control for hard real-time systems. final report NSC 85-2213-E-309-001, National Science Council, 1997.

[10] L. Shu and M. Young. Real-time concurrency control with analytic worst-case latency guarantees. In *Proceedings of the 10th IEEE Workshop on Real-Time Operating Systems and Software*, pages 69–73, New York, N.Y., May 1993.

[11] L. Shu and M. Young. A mixed locking/abort protocol for hard real-time systems. In *Proc. of the 11th IEEE workshop on real-time operating systems and software*, pages 102–106, May 1994.

[12] L. Shu, M. Young, and R. Rajkumar. An abort-ceiling protocol for controlling priority inversion. In *Proc. of the 1st international workshop on real-time computing systems and applications*, Oct. 1994.

[13] J. Stankovic, K. Shin, H. Kopetz, K. Ramamritham, L. Sha, D. Locke, J. Liu, A. Mok, S. Davidson, I. Lee, and J. Strosnider. Real-time computing: A critical enabling technology. http://cs-www.bu.edu/ftp/IEEE-RTTC/public/rtfunding.ps.

[14] J. A. Stankovic. Real-time computing systems: The next generation. In J. A. Stankovic and K. Ramamritham, editors, *Hard Real-Time Systems*, chapter 2, pages 14–38. IEEE Computer Society Press, 1988.

[15] J. Voelcker. How computers helped stampede the stock market. *IEEE SPECTRUM*, pages 30–33, December 1987.

[16] J. Zachman. A framework for information systems architecture. *IBM Systems Journal*, pages 276–292, 1987.

[17] J. Zalewski. Questionnaire on real-time systems education. http://cs-www.bu.edu/ftp/IEEE-RTTC/public/questionnaire.ascii.

[18] J. Zalewski. Cohesive use of commercial tools in a classroom. In *Proc. of 7th SEI CSEE conference*, pages 65–75, Jan. 1994.

Real-Time Systems Education
at the University of Colorado-Denver

Marty Humphrey
Department of Computer Science and Engineering
University of Colorado at Denver
Denver, Colorado 80217
humphrey@cse.cudenver.edu

1 Introduction

This short paper describes the efforts of a newly-graduated, first-year Assistant Professor toward designing and developing a graduate-level course in Real-Time Systems. Section 2 contains a description of the course and its students. Section 3 presents an evaluation of the course (by its instructor). This section includes comments on changes that could be made and comments on what is lacking in the course.

2 The Course

The initial design of the course centered on lecture notes of a graduate real-time system course at the University of Massachusetts at Amherst, taught by Jack Stankovic. These lecture notes primarily consisted of a collection of research papers presented in the class. Additionally, I intended to use course topics of another graduate-level course in Real-Time Systems taught at UMass-Amherst by Mani Krishna, which I had also taken. At the time that I was putting the class together, I did not feel there was an appropriate textbook available for the class. However, upon learning of a new textbook by Mani Krishna and Kang Shin, I readily adopted that book at the class text. The book title is "Real-Time Systems", published by McGraw-Hill [1].

Eight Masters-level students signed up for the course (our department does not have a PhD program). The students in our program can be characterized as focused, mature students often holding a full-time job. Therefore, the students did not have ample time for the course; however, the time that they put toward the course tended to be very concentrated and effective.

The course was designed such that the first 12 weeks were lecture-style; the remaining class time was used for student presentations. The lectures covered in the class consisted of roughly the first seven chapters of the book. These topics are: introduction, characterizing real-time systems and tasks, task assignment and scheduling, programming languages and tools, real-time databases, real-time communication, and fault-tolerant techniques. Generally, the lecture material did not differ much from the text. The notable differences were an in-depth discussion of the analysis of pipelines on the calculation of WCET [5] and an in-depth discussion of the Spring kernel [4].

In the three weeks devoted to student presentations, students presented recent papers not covered by the Krishna and Shin textbook. These topics included processor capacity reserves, QoS architectures, multimedia OSs, certain real-time communication protocols, and the "group paper" for the ACM 50th anniversary issue [3].

The sole prerequisite of the course was an undergraduate operating systems class. The course requirements were to read the materials, participate in class discussions, present one paper, write one short paper on current research, and write one program. The program was based on an assignment given in Jack Stankovic's class at UMass-Amherst, which was to design and write a fixed-priority scheduling simulation, using different protocols for the management of resources (FCFS, EDF, priority inheritance, and priority ceiling). That is, the students were expected to write a simulation of multiple processes requiring multiple resources, and to use a variety of different policies to manage those resources. Additionally, the students were told to "evaluate" their algorithms. Vague terms were used to allow the students to determine for themselves what exactly comprised an evaluation.

3 Course Evaluation and Lessons Learned

I originally designed the course to introduce and survey the implications of time-dependent computation of the fundamental areas of computer systems science, such as compilers, operating systems, programming languages, and architecture. However, it was apparent fairly quickly that approximately half of the students would have preferred a course that emphasized embedded systems (as perhaps presented in Laplante's textbook [2]). Upon learning this, I chose to modify the course content slightly to discuss embedded systems whenever appropriate, but without dropping the original intended topics (it should be pointed out that the class was clearly advertised with my original goals).

I found the text book presented most topics well, so I envision using the text book for the next incarnation of the class. A particularly appealing feature of the book is that it includes mathematical proofs for many of the scheduling results. While I did not directly present many of these proofs, the students were always encouraged to decipher them on their own time. In other words, the book readily presents advanced topics for motivated students.

When I designed the course, I hoped to get a few students who could share first-hand experiences with real-time systems. That is, the graduate Computer Science and Engineering students at the University of Colorado at Denver generally work in industry; it was only logical that they might be able to provide direct experiences. Unfortunately, most of the students did not have appreciable direct experience. The few that did could not discuss their projects because of proprietary concerns.

The assignment to design, write, and evaluate a fixed-priority scheduling system was not very successful, primarily because I found that the students did not have a thorough understanding of the manipulation of queues within the operating system, upon which to base their simulation. While the students had all taken an under-grad OS class (generally at different colleges and universities), the "completeness" of these classes were not equivalent. Some students did not quite understand the movement of threads between various queues when attempting to acquire semaphores. In order for the students to attempt the assignment, a substantial refresher was needed in operating system scheduling mechanism. The more serious problem, however, was that the students did not appreciate the open-ended nature of the evaluation—they wanted to be told exactly how to run their simulation, exactly what to measure, and exactly how to plot/characterize their results. I don't feel that this is a limitation of our particular students; perhaps it is a limitation of graduate students who are not inclined toward "research". Eventually the students figured out how to perform the evaluation, but not until I had given them ample suggestions.

The assignment to write a paper required the students to, essentially, choose a topic we discussed in class and find and analyze more recent research in the area related to the topic. The students had some initial problems with this, because, quite simply, many of them had never been asked to perform "research". I knew this before the assignment was given; certainly one goal of the assignment was to make the students learn how to do this (by either using the Web or by looking at proceedings of the more recent conferences, such as RTSS and RTAS). The papers turned in by the students were certainly acceptable, given that researching topics was a new activity to most students.

The students in general were very interested in the materials. This, in part, leads me to conclude that they were better served by this type of course, rather than "how to build embedded systems". Students participated in class discussions. They had the most difficulty with some of the more formal topics, such as scheduling proofs and formal methods.

The students' evaluations of the course yielded some interesting observations. First, some questioned the approach of organizing the course as a "survey", and would have preferred a more in-depth treatment of some of the materials. Students indicated that they enjoyed the chance to research a particular topic and present the material to the class. However, the majority of the class indicated that a more hands-on approach would have been more valuable for this subject. Specifically, a real-time lab in which students could experience the design of a real-time system (with a close link between hardware and software required of real-time systems) would have been very valuable.

Therefore, first and foremost, it is important that the course have better student projects. Unfortunately, I have not been able to find projects given the resources available for the department and the campus. In addition, being a new faculty member, I have had little time to devote to such concerns, as I become acclimated to my new surroundings. In the future, efforts will be made to connect to the substantial local industry in Denver, to both better ground the topics in the course, and perhaps develop a real-time laboratory specifically for the class.

References

[1] C.M. Krishna and Kang Shin. *Real-Time Systems*. McGraw-Hill, New York, 1997.

[2] Phillip A. Laplante. *Real-Time Systems Design and Analysis: An Engineer's Handbook*. IEEE Computer Science Society Press, New York, 1993.

[3] John A. Stankovic. Real-time and embedded systems. *ACM 50th Anniversary Report on Real-Time Computing Research*, 1997.

[4] John A. Stankovic and Krithi Ramamritham. The Spring kernel: A new paradigm for real-time systems. *IEEE Software*, 8(3):62–72, May 1991.

[5] N. Zhang, A. Burns, and M. Nicholson. Pipeline processors and worst-case execution times. *Real-Time Systems*, 5(4), October 1993.

Chapter 2

Methods and Tools for Teaching Real-Time Systems

Engineering the Real-Time Teaching Process?

J.-J. Schwarz (*), R. Aubry, J. Skubich.
L3i, Département Informatique B502
Institut National des Sciences Appliquées de Lyon
69621 Villeurbanne Cedex France
e-mail {jjs I aubry I skubich}@if.insa-lyon.fr
(*) IUT A Département Informatique UCB Lyon1
69622 Villeurbanne Cedex France.

Abstract

This paper gives information about Real-Time Teaching at the Department of Informatics at the National Institute of Applied Sciences (INSA) de Lyon. The first part of the paper describes how teaching (and thus real-time teaching) is seen as an engineering process, and how real-time teaching is related to the other computer science domains. The second part gives an overview of the specific Real-Time courses.

1. Introduction

In a previous paper [SCH 96] a rather complete presentation of our Institute had been made, we will therefore confine ourselves to presenting its main features. The National Institute of Applied Sciences (INSA) of LYON is a Higher Education School of Engineering which belongs to the network of French «Grandes Ecoles d'Ingénieurs». The mission of INSA is three-fold : engineering education, research and technology transfer, and continuing education. The student/teacher ratio is rather low and allows the teacher to transmit not only knowledge but also experience. Most of the lecturers are researchers and maintain their post for a long period of time (this gives the pedagogical team time for long-term projects).

INSA is a Polytechnic Institute including nine departments of specialization where the students have to attend, after a two-year curriculum dedicated to math, physics, ..., a three- year specialized curriculum before graduation. As far as the Department of Informatics is concerned, a generalist education has been chosen : equal importance is given to each domain of informatics, and a greater significance is given to requirement analysis, specification and design methods rather than to implementation techniques. So, students are taught to be designers and architects and are therefore placed in a semi-professionnal environment where they deal with projects of increasing complexity which are carried out in the frame of teamwork.

2. Teaching: an engineering process ?

Education can be seen as an engineering process [PAU 93], [DOR 93] presenting strong analogies with the development process of a software product [ISO 12207] within the frame of a total quality approach [CRO 79]. This process (Fig. 1.) may be considered as a kind of manufacturing process (in carefully chosen sentences and with all the respect due to our students) the aim of which is, starting from a more or less homogenous student-input flow, to educate engineers with a required level of qualification. It is associated to a continuous improvement process which implies regularly the content of the teaching according to significant technological or economical changes.

It takes about five years, between the moment the decision is taken to set up the new modalities of the educating process and the moment the earliest validations are made thanks to consultations, by means of polls, of our former students (2 and 5 years after their graduation), which allow us to observe the requirement evolutions.

The educating process being itself dynamic, the system is always under transient response mode : specification is continuously changing and therefore, at a given time, the results of the process no longer correspond to the specification which has generated them.

Concerning the duration of the life-cycle, the specification phase can be considered relatively short if a good and permanent knowledge of the employment situation is known. A major difficulty lies on the one hand (and this is a specificity of education in Computer

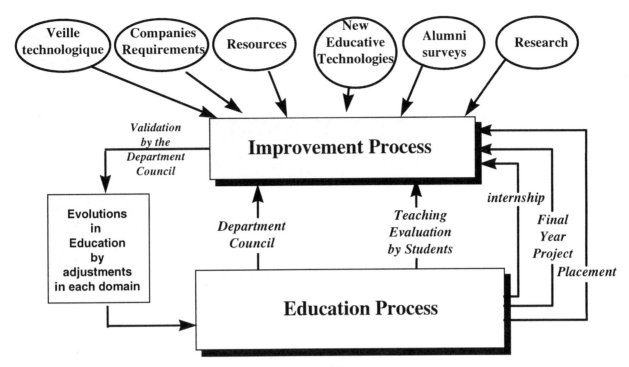

Figure 1. Flows in the Education process

Science) in the possibility to choose between the actual requirements and fashion conformance, and on the other hand in deciding when large changes are modifying the process design.

As the process is a lengthy one, intermediate « test-points » (quality control) have to be introduced. For this purpose, as far as we are concerned, internships play the role of a feedback function by getting a measurement, a kind of distance measurement between the content of the training and what is actually used or asked for within a company (even if these internships are mandatory for our students, the related work itself is not assessed). Consequently we have the possibility of a quasi-continuous monitoring (at least, we hope so !) of the actual situation of the industrial world and therefore adjustments can be made. Thus Each pedagogical team monitors the technological development within its related domain (information systems, operating systems and networks, industrial computing and scientific computing).

This approach implies looking for fixed points, invariants, technology-independence and then proceeding by successive refinements to learn state-of-the-art techniques. The deepening of the knowledge in specific techniques for a given domain is done when all the basis have been experienced.

These general principles apply to each the former mentioned domains, and obviously also to the industrial field.

Training in real-time is integrated in the more general domain of « industrial computing ». The quality of the design (and its documentation) and architecture features are highlighted and the concerned training has been designed in order to progressively approach more and more complex projects and teamwork organization.

Because our teaching is essentially based on projects, the part of the time devoted to lectures is relatively small. Currently these lectures consist in the presentation of a specification method and design tools dedicated to the use of standard real-time multitasking executives. The aim is to stress on the methodology rather than on the technicality of the final solution.

This teaching, which takes place in the second year of specialization, and which is project-based with only few lectures, supposes nevertheless that student's knowledge relies on a sound basis in the different fields of computer science. In order to get this, it is necessary to establish a strong dialogue between the corresponding pedagogical teams. This good grounding that we demand can be split into three classes : the knowledge we (the « industrial computing » pedagogical team) « inherit » from the closely related domains, the knowledge we share with others and finally the knowledge which is specific to our teaching.

- ***Inherited* knowledge.**

It is naturally essential that our students have a good grip on Algorithmics and Programming. Therefore, the initiation into Programming of (small) real-time applications starts only after a semester of training in algorithms and programming languages like C and C++.

29

- *Shared* **knowledge.**

The «Computer Architecture» course, which could be entitled « From the component to the system », is linked to industrial computing and it is performed in a close co-operation and synchronization with the « Operating Systems » course. The approach is down-up going from the description of the elementary components of a computer to the mechanisms for the support of the realization of operating systems (multitasking issues, memory management, interrupt and exception handling, mutual exclusion, ...).

The « Operating Systems » course follows a top-down approach starting from the use of the UNIX system at an operator level to the multitasking system programming level. Both approaches meet themselves at a given point from which the students can have two different viewpoints of the same problematic. For example, questions raised from the development of a device driver are seen in both lectures, but the carrying out of such a driver occurs during a real-time project. This part is also the opportunity to handle a cross-development tool with debugging facilities for assembly and C programs.

The same sort of co-operation links us with the « Networking » pedagogical team (almost all real-time applications involve now networking issues). During the first term, students are essentially trained with the lowest layers (physical layer, data link layer) of the OSI model. Experience is gained during a common project where these layers are seen in conjunction with input-output interfacing techniques, and students are made aware of the overlapping areas between real-time programming and networking.

The transport layer (level 4) is the subject of two separated projects : the first one specific to networking techniques and which deals with the internal protocol of the layer, and the second one is a real-time project in which the use of the transport layer services of Intel Multibus II is required in a multiprocessor application.

- *Specific* **Knowledge.**

As previously mentioned our basic teaching particular to the real time domain for the realization of the projects, deals with a specification method and a design method. The specification method is SART which is, despite all its drawbacks (lack of verification tools), a standard in Industry : a lot of CASE tools exist proposing this method and gradually some temporal validation tools are emerging (see [FRA 97] in these proceedings).

At the design level, although we are only using off-the-shelf real time executives, we were eager to introduce a good abstraction level against all the particularities of a given operating system. So, for training purposes, we developed the graphical design language LACATRE. The reader will find more details about this language and its use as a method in [SCH 96].

However, it is now undeniable that the object oriented technology is becoming mature, and of course a debate has been initiated on the necessity to set up (now or a bit later) this technology.

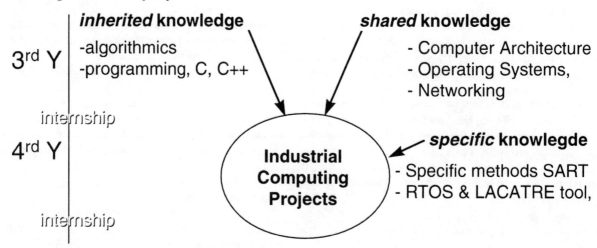

Figure 2. Knowledge for Real Time Teaching

3. Advanced Techniques

Advanced techniques adapted to real-time programming are mainly discussed during the last year of studies by means of optional courses and especially within the « Real-Time Architecture » course of the postgraduate diploma curriculum attended by students wanting to carry on research (PhD) or simply wanting to have some additional education to a first contact with research. Optional courses deal mainly with distributed systems, dependability, project development in ADA, and some of these courses are taught by foreign lecturers.

The « Real-Time Architecture » postgraduate course, follows a down-up approach starting from the problematic of time and ending at systems which integrate time as a validation parameter of an application. The principle of this course relies on the idea of basing each of its chapters on one or more fundamental research papers. For example, the chapter devoted to scheduling starts with a complete discussion of the seminal paper of Liu and Layland [LIU 73] where the fundamental theorems of scheduling are demonstrated.

Time, Clocks and synchronization mechanisms.

It is rather difficult, not surprisingly, to explain the concept of time [HOO 91]. In this chapter, we try to make the concept clear, relying on a historical basis, showing how humans deal with time either by ignoring it (as it has been the case for a long time in Computer Science) or by attempting to perceive it by trying to measure it.

Some time is spent tracing the history of the different kinds of clocks developed during the last millennia, and we conclude with the current use of UTC time with the leap seconds consequences.

Time measurement by means of a local clock leads quickly to synchronization issues in distributed (multi processes) systems where each process has its own clock. This part is illustrated with Lamport's papers [LAM 78], dealing as well with the normal functioning (requesting messages between processes to piggyback timestamps) as with the synchronization in the presence of faults (fail-silent or byzantine) [LAM 85].

Real-Time Systems and their environment (Spatial and temporal interfaces).

Hard-real time and soft real-time are characterized as precisely as possible. The given definitions are then completed with the explanation of some misconcepts about Real Time with ideas extracted from the well known paper by Stankovic [STA 88].

A real-time application is, by nature, strongly coupled to the external environment. This implies that the spatial as well as temporal interfaces, have to be precisely defined. Spatial interfaces (data) are mainly treated through the temporal features of the input-output management (DA/AD converters, DMA management, caching and buffering issues).

The temporal interface is the opportunity to introduce two viewpoints which lead later to the two-often-opposed paradigms: Event Trigged systems and Time Trigged systems with temporal firewalls. The discussion gets its matter from papers by Kopetz [KOP 93].

The chapter ends with a focus given to a good specification of these interfaces especially thanks to the use of the RSM (Requirement States Machines) [JAF 91]. This method can be considered as very efficient as an assistant to the specification of inputs and outputs of a real-time system.

Scheduling.

This part is a very classical one and consists, starting from the first results of Liu and Layland [LIU 73], in reviewing the most significant scheduling protocols (and their prerequisites) derived from Rate Monotonic and Earliest Deadline algorithms : scheduling periodic tasks, scheduling with sporadic tasks, resolution of the priority inversion when tasks share common resources.

Distributed Applications and Fieldbuses.

The strictly software features of distributed applications are exposed in a course, which is specific to distributed systems, during which the basic issues of distributed systems are developed, and where the main off-the-shelves and lab-grown operating systems are described. We bring additional information on real-time oriented operating systems (Spring [STA 91], HART [SHI 91], MARS [DAM 89] and on the importance of networking characteristics in the field of distributed applications. At this level, focus is given to the MAC (Medium Access Level) sub-layer because of its direct influence on the temporal predictability of message delivery. We obviously describe TDMA techniques, but we also give particular mention to the techniques involved in various fieldbuses. This chapter follows the one related to scheduling because it becomes interesting to exhibit some parallelism between task scheduling on a processor and temporal ordering of messages on network.

Design and Specification of Real-Time Applications.

During the projects of the second year of specialization, the design of applications has been seen from the practical point of view of problem solving with emphasis on software quality criteria. We now give a more formal consistency, strongly insisting more on the predictability of the behaviour of programs and their correctness verification. Concerning the asynchronous model of realization (multitasking), we use our LACATRE environment [SCH 96] to show how it is possible to carry out correctness verification on the different running phases of an application by translating automatically a LACATRE graphical design to a formalism better suited to verification. For the synchronous model, we present an introduction to the ESTEREL language [BER 85].

As far as these formal validation techniques are concerned, we made the choice of those where the formalism is rather simple (« human understandable » for the average designer) and nevertheless potentially efficient. So, Shaw's CRSM (Communicating Real time State Machines) [SHA 92] and RTL (Real Time Logic) [JAH 86] are subjects to particular developments.

4. Conclusion

Our teaching approach of real-time takes place within the frame of the Education of generalist engineers which puts forward project-based learning and teamwork. After the students awareness of the solving of complex problems, we give the possibility to those of them who want to carry on this field to proceed by refinement for the deepening of their knowledge.

In order to aim at a better conceptualization (and therefore to get a better control) of the Education process, we attempt to consider it as a classical engineering process with its own life cycle. More than ever, it is necessary for us to take into account, as in other manufacturing or industrial fields, efficiency and quality for the brand image of our product criteria.

The Department of Informatics is currently in a brain storming phase on the global education process, and the pedagogical team involved in real-time training is also questioning the evolution of this training. The discussions and the talks, which have be given on the occasion of this workshop are bringing also an interesting contribution to our meditations.

References

[BER 85] Berry G., Gonthier G., "The synchronous programming language ESTEREL, design, semantics, implementation". TR 327, INRIA France, 1985.

[CRO 79] Crosby P.B, *"Quality is Free"*, Mc Graw-Hill, New York, NY,1979.

[DAM 89] Damm A., Reisinger J., Schwabl W. and Kopetz H.. "The real-time operating system of MARS". ACM Oper. Syst. Rev. V23 N3, Jul. 1989, pp 141-157.

[DOR 93] Dorling, *"SPICE(Software Process Improvement and evaluation) "*, In the Programme and Abstract Book for sofware modelling in Practice, Butterworth-Heineman, Oxford

[FRA 97] France R. B., *"Towards Practical Formal Modeling Techniques for Complex Systems"*. 2nd IEEE Real Time Education Workshop. Montreal, June 97.

[HOO 91] Hoogeboom B., Halang W.A., *"The concept of time in software engineering for real-time systems"*. 3rd I.C. software Engineering for Real Time Systems., IEE Conference Pub. N344, pp 156-163.

[ISO 12207] ISO 12207., Joint Technical Committee, ISO /IEC/JTC1, Information technology, Subcommittee SC 7, Software engineering.

[JAF 91] Jaffe M. S., Leveson N. G., Heimdahl M.P.E. and Melhart B.E., *"Software Requirements Analysis for Real-Time Process-Control Systems"*., IEEE TSE V17 N3, Mar 1991., pp 241-258.

[JAH 86] Jahanian F., Mok A.K., *"Safety analysis of timing properties in real-time systems"*. IEEE Trans. Soft. Eng. V12 N9, Sep 1986. pp 890-904.

[KOP 93] Kopetz H., *"Should Responsive Systems be Event-Triggered or Time-Triggered?"*. IEICE Trans. Inf. & Syst. Vol E76-D, N11, November 1993, pp 1325-1332.

[LAM 78] Lamport l., *"Time, Clocks and the Ordering of Events in a Distributed System"*, Comm. ACM, V 21 N7, July 1978, pp 559-565.

[LAM 85] Lamport L., Melliar-Smith P.M., *"Synchronizing clocks in the presence of faults"*. J. ACM. V32 N1, Jan. 1985, pp 52-78.

[LIU 73] Liu C. L., Layland J. W., *"Scheduling Algorithms for Multiprogramming in a Hard Realtime Environment"*. J. ACM., Feb. 1973, pp 46-61.

[PAU 93] Paulk M.C. et al, *"Capability Maturity Model for Software, Version 1.1"*, Tech. report CMU/SEI-93-TR624, Software Eng. Inst., Pittsburgh,1993

[SHA 92] Shaw A., *"Communicating Real-Time State Machines"*., IEEE TSE. V15 N7., 1992, pp 805-816.

[SCH 96] Schwarz J. J., Skubich J., Maranzana M. and Aubry R.. *"Graphical Programming and Real-Time Design Instruction"*. 1st IEEE Workshop on Real-Time Systems Education (RTSE 96), Daytona Beach, Florida, Apr 1996.

[SHI 91] Shin K. G. "HARTS : a distributed Real-Time Architecture"., IEEE Computer, V24 N5, May 1991, pp 25-35.

[STA 88] Stankovic J. A., "Misconceptions about real-time computing : a serious problem for the next-generation systems". IEEE Computer., V21 N10, Oct. 1988, pp 10-19.

[STA 91] Stankovic J.A., Ramamritham K., *"The SPRING Kernel: a new paradigm for Real Time Systems"*., IEEE Software V8 N3, May 1991, pp 62-72.

Impact of Quality Systems on Real-Time Software Lectures and Laboratories

G. Motet*, R. Fleurquin**, T. Szmuc***

* GERII/LESIA, DGEI/INSA, Complexe Scientifique de Rangueil, 31077 Toulouse cedex 4, France, motet@dge.insa-tlse.fr
** IUT Vannes, Kercado, BP 561, 56017 Vannes cedex, France, Regis.Fleurquin@iu-vannes.fr
*** Institute of Automatics, University of Mining and Metallurgy, al. Mickiewicza 30, 30-059 Krakow, Poland, tsz@ia.agh.edu.pl

Abstract

Even though everyone agrees that many scientific domains must be used by engineers to develop systems, these domains are today presented to the students through different lectures. The subjects dealt with may however influence each other. In this paper, we describe the impact of the Quality domain on the Real-Time Software education domain. We show how advances in "Quality Policies" can improve the teaching of Real-Time Software. This concerns both lectures and laboratories.

Certain aspects concerning Real-Time Software education presented in this paper were studied within the framework of the European project TEMPUS No. 96129 (CCATIE). Research on Quality Policies was conducted in the GERII research group of the LESIA laboratory at INSA.

1. Initial statement: Quality Check

1.1 Inventory

Six years ago, Real-Time was taught in the DGEI (Department of Electrical Engineering and Computer Sciences) of INSA (National Institute of Applied Sciences) in Toulouse, describing the technological means allowing real-time applications to be implemented. The lectures on software technology mainly described the real-time features of the Ada language. The implementation of the Run-Time System Environment was also described, focusing on the Real-Time Kernel in charge of task management. The hardware implementation technology concerned the functionalities of the microprocessors and other components, such as the Programmable Interrupt Controller, the timers, etc.

However, the results of the real-time software technology lectures were not satisfactory, even if the students appreciated the lectures, considering the task management capabilities as original. The problems were especially perceptible in the laboratories. Design faults were numerous and detections and corrections were very complex and time-consuming. Many students spent many additional hours in an attempt to obtain correct executable software, whereas others completed their work quickly. Some students never obtained a correct program in spite of the many efforts made. Most students got the impression therefore that the time required to obtain correct executable real-time software depended only on the degree of luck of the designer. This impression was strengthened by the behavior of the program esteemed as non-deterministic (and sometimes hazardous) by students trained to develop sequential systems.

At first, we reacted by laying stress on programming style, giving lectures on this subject and using documents such as the version of [21] available at that time. The aim of this was to reduce faults associated with misunderstanding the program or to detect these faults making the program easier to review. We then reinforced our lectures on the other fault detection techniques [18]. But honestly, the results were inconclusive.

1.2 Quality Check

At this time, the teaching technique considered the development process as a "black box" on which no actions could be performed. The correctness of the executable program was assessed a posteriori. When a failure occurred at run-time, the associated fault was detected and the program modified, and so on, until a correct program was obtained.

Consequently, total development time was very long and could not be predicted. Moreover, the dependability of the final software was not assured and, sometimes, a correct program was never obtained.

Such a statement recognizes the poor **External Quality** of the program. Indeed, the notion of External Quality is defined by:

- *high dependability*: the services provided by the software system must be safe and the system user must be able to rely on them;
- *short production duration*: in particular, the real-time program must be completed before a specified deadline;
- *low cost*: in our case, the cost is measured by the time spent by the students.

For industrial real-time applications, external quality is fundamental, due to the important tasks entrusted to software in operation (flight and traffic control of aircraft, anti-lock braking systems on cars, supervision of nuclear power plants, etc.) and due to economical constraints. However, the real-time systems developed by the students did not reach such a quality level. The reasons must be examined.

Concerning quality, the software development approach presented is called **Quality Check**. This was the first **Quality Policy** introduced. Let us recall that a "Quality Policy is the overall intentions and directions of an organization as regards quality" [13]. Here, the Quality Policy consists in judging the functional correctness of an executable real-time program after it has been produced. Note that this Quality Policy deals partially with the dependability of the program, that is, "the reliance which can justifiably be placed in the services provided by the designed software" [15]. However, this policy does not consider time and cost.

The practical means used to implement a Quality Policy (that is, reach the goals) comprise a **Quality System**. In our case, these means concern behavioral testing techniques.

The Quality Check policy used had perverse effects on the students' work. They justified the botching up of the production of the first version of the program by statements such as "I must obtain the first version as soon as possible because I will have to spend a lot of time debugging it".

Moreover, the evaluation of the student's work is limited to the executing the program by test sequences which progressively check increasingly complex behaviors of the software. Other teaching aspects were thus not judged. For instance, the students justified the poor quality of the programming style by statements such as "The laboratory is for *real-time software* and not *programming quality*".

2. First improvement: Quality Control

2.1 Inventory

The unacceptable statement is due to the fact that the lectures focused on the product (the real-time program) whereas the students' two difficulties were related to the process used to obtain this product:

- the software failures are not due to the software program itself. Software does not grow old like electronic components if maintenance and dependencies on the execution means are not considered [17]. Failures only come from design faults, that is, faults in the designer's reasoning;
- the long development time (and the high cost involved) are due to the difficulty the designer has in mastering his/her creation.

The contents of the lectures were thus changed to place the accent on the development process. These modifications successively took into account the 3 phases of evolution which occurred in the *Quality Control policy*.

2.2 The three phases in the Quality Control policy progress

2.2.1 Process structuring

We first introduced a structuring of the development process. The process was split into a sequence of defined activities with specified goals. We considered the conventional "V cycle" (requirements, specification, design, etc.). The process was split to reduce the gap between the problem and its solution (the program), making several small steps instead of one large one.

The students clearly understood the theoretical interests of these steps. However, during the laboratories they were unable to provide a solution for each step of the given problem. In fact, they were confused because the lecture on real-time software was suddenly dealing with the development process whereas they had been trained to handle software products.

2.2.2 Standardized languages

To solve this problem, the second change consisted in introducing standardized languages (also called models or modeling means) allowing the result of each step to be expressed. For instance, the system specification was described using Petri nets. This made the student's work easier. Indeed, each step then referred to a language, that is, something associated with the software product.

We also hoped that the use of standardized means of expression would facilitate the use of review techniques. This would have been possible because the students were working in pairs during the laboratories. We gave them advice on sharing out the work and checking the result proposed by the other person, the review techniques being very efficient [7]. But, at time of writing, the method is not a success, the students being unable to share out their activities.

However, thanks to standard languages, tools were used to detect faults introduced during each step. For instance, the Petri net model allows deadlocks or undesirable state reachability to be highlighted [16].

Now, at the end of each step, and not only when the executable program is completed, the students produce a document containing the model produced as the result of this step. The assessments of the students are therefore better but the time spent by the teacher to do these assessments is longer.

The described techniques concern *vertical means*. More recently, we introduced two *horizontal means*, that is, means useful for globally managing the project: project planning and documentation management. However, the students did not perceive the interest of such means as only short times are required in the laboratories. Unfortunately, these activities must be carried out, especially when real-time software is concerned, as real-time applications often have very long lives. For example, the software embedded in an Airbus aircraft is maintained for 15 to 20 years. Maintenance costs are therefore high.

2.2.3 Measurements

The last improvement added to the Quality Control policy consisted in systematically obtaining measurements on the process and on the products it generates: software size, cost of each phase, number of faults, etc.. This allows costs, duration and dependability to be predicted when a new project is started. However, this aspect was not explained in the lectures because it was impossible to put it into practice in the laboratories as the students were developing only one real-time application. Consequently, they had no experience from previous real-time software developments.

3. Second improvement: Quality Assurance

3.1 Principle

Even if the step-by-step realization, expressing successive models by means of standardized languages, is easier than the direct production of a real-time program, the students struggled with the problem to be solved at each step. Obtaining a correct solution for a step seemed to be dependent on experience that they did not possess. They again considered that this lack of experience could only be compensated for by a certain degree of luck. However, developments made by an experienced designer are not due to good luck. He/she knows the way to reach the solution. We analyzed this statement as follows:

1. The language used to express the solution of a step offers features. These features are proposed by the creator of the model because he/she considered them as "well adapted". This term expresses the fact that these features are suitable for taking the requirements characterizing the studied domain into account. For instance, the task concept was introduced to express a solution for the design step. This feature is useful for taking the "independency of reactions to the occurrence of events" into account. This last statement is one of the requirements characterizing the design of real-time systems.

2. So, our lectures on real-time software must not focus on the features offered by the languages but on the requirements which characterize the domain. In our case, during the lectures, we successively consider as domains: the requirements of real-time systems, the specifications of real-time systems, the design of real-time systems, the programming of real-time systems, etc.. We will now show how the features of the selected language provide a solution for these requirements. We will call the reasoning to pass from one requirement to one feature (or several features) the "rule".

3. One development step consists in translating a model of a program described by means of the features of a first language into a model correlating features of a second language. To obtain a solution for this step, the designer must analyze the requirements appearing in the problem handled (that is, the first model). He/she must then deduce the features composing the solution (that is, the second model) by using the rules. For instance, the design step must start by

analyzing the dependency relationships relevant to taking the events, existing in the specification text of the treated problem, into account. Thus tasks are deduced.

A lot of work was done to analyze the requirements characterizing each step and their associations with features provided by models. We cannot develop this subject in this paper. This will be done in a book which will be published in the near future.

This approach was presented during lectures. Initially, it was perceived by the students as philosophical. This was due to the fact that the students were trained to reason on systems and not on the development process that they use to produce these systems. However, several practical examples using the proposed process increased their confidence. Even if they still considered the ideas as abstract, they also considered that the "method worked efficiently".

3.2 Quality Assurance

We then propose rules to be applied to perform each step in the development.
1. These rules are given to the students.
2. They must use them during the development in laboratories.
3. They must justify that the rules were applied. For instance, in the design document, they must justify each task or each synchronization mechanism, explaining their analysis of the characteristics of the specification model and the rules used.

Here, we find the 3 principles of **Quality Assurance**: "Write what you do", "Do what is written", "Prove that you did it".

Quality Assurance ensures to the client (here the lecturer) that the developer (here the student) masters the real-time software creation process.

Thanks to Quality Assurance, the client can check compliance with the rules. Thus, the examination of the documents supplied by the student requires a lot of time but gives quite a good idea on the student's understanding.

Also, one may be afraid that the additional work done by the students would increase the development time. This does not happen as:
- the use of rigorous procedures and rules avoids errors (fault prevention);
- the writing of the justifications allows a check to be done by the students (fault detection);
- as the solution produced is correct, there is no need to spend time debugging. For instance, it is well known that the time spent to avoid a fault in the

specifications is less that the time required to correct it after its detection at run-time [2].

An anecdote can be given. The students develop a small real-time software application in laboratories during 6 sessions of 3 hours each. Generally, at the end of the fifth session, the students have not produced an executable program; they are completing the programming with Ada. During the first year of this new method, tension was high at the beginning of the sixth session. After an hour, one student shouted out "It works!". We explained that, for us, this was quite normal. The non-quality of a real-time software, not its quality, is abnormal. The students were skeptical, we gave them the following example: assume that you are the manager of the team developing the software embedded into a new aircraft (such an activity is done in Toulouse by Aerospatiale for Airbus Industrie); the first flight is today; you are in the airport control tower; the aircraft takes off and the flight goes off without problems. Now imagine the face of the pilot when he/she hears you say in his headset: "we are lucky, the software works!".

4. Future step: Quality Management

Recent Quality Policies are called "**Quality Management**". Previously, we used a fixed Quality System. Quality Management consists in introducing *continuous improvement* of the Quality System in order to permanently improve the development process and thus the quality of the software produced.

Today, no practices associated with Quality Management are introduced into the lectures on Real-Time Software. We are studying how we can do this.

Firstly, we studied PIP (Process Improvement Programs) introduced to obtain this continuous improvement. Industrial use of these programs to develop real-time applications seems to be very interesting. For example, results were given by firms such as Hughes Aircraft [10], OMRON Corporation [20], Raytheon [5], Schlumberger [22], Texas Instruments [1], US Air Force [4]. Studies concerning several companies are also given in [9], [3] and [8].

Two difficulties must be considered in applying these programs to education:
1. these programs are based on the fact that several applications are developed. In our case, only one real-time application is designed in the laboratories;
2. these programs were generally developed for big companies whereas two students comprise a micro-firm.

Concerning this last problem, we studied Process Improvement Programs customized for small firms [14] and we proposed a new one [6]. Today, for Real-Time Software development education purposes, we think that the PSP proposed by Humphrey [11], [12] seems to be a good basis to elaborate a suitable program.

5. Conclusion

In this last section, we will draw some conclusions on the evolution of Real-Time Software education at INSA to take the Quality requirements associated with this kind of software into account. We will give two options: those for the students and those for the lecturers.

5.1 Students' viewpoints

First and foremost, the students' productivity was increased. The great majority of students were able to perform the required work during the sessions. Others spent a few additional hours.

The time required to perform each step changed gradually. Today, they spend a lot of time on the specification phase. This is normal for real-time systems [19]. However, debugging is now negligible. The importance of the specifications had another interesting effect: no students produced programs which did not meet requirements. During the previous years, around 10% of the students did not completely understand the requirements described for a given subject.

Moreover, the students now have a new opinion of their future jobs. As previously pointed out, the non-deterministic behavior of the real-time applications (compared with sequential systems) reinforced the idea that hazard was the critical factor in obtaining correct software. Now, the students understand that the correction of a real-time software application only depends on the mastering of the development process.

At the beginning, the strictness of the process (steps, rules, documents, etc.) was considered very difficult by the students. Indeed, a lot of them previously considered the development of real-time software as an exciting hobby whereas it is a very serious job. In particular, the presentation of the method which consists in deducing the features used from the analyzed requirements, must be illustrated with many examples during the lectures. The methodological aspects are not really appreciated by the students. The laboratories are also very important because it is the only real opportunity that the students have to try out this method.

Finally, the students are also very interested in the use of multiple knowledge, learnt during separate lectures and necessary to develop real-time software applications:

Software Engineering, CASE, Quality, Petri nets, OMT, Ada, Dependability.

5.2 Lecturers' viewpoints

The lecturers participating in the changes made in real-time software education consider that the work is now harder than before.

Firstly, the lectures presenting methodological concepts require more preparation as the students are not trained to acquire such knowledge.

Secondly, the examination of the real-time applications developed by the students now requires a lot of time. As we pointed out, initially a test sequence activating increasingly complex behaviors of the application easily allowed a grade to be given. However, the value provided assessed one real-time software application and not directly the student's knowledge in the real-time software domain. The introduction of development steps made the examination of the intermediary models necessary (specification, design, programming, test sequences). This work was made harder still when the justifications were added.

Another point of view is quite interesting: that of the other colleagues. On the one hand, the use of many other lectures to develop real-time software arouses the students' interest in other domains. This is appreciated by the lecturers concerned. On the other hand, much opposition was put up (and is still being put up) against the methodological aspects. We heard statements such as "a method cannot be explained, it must be acquired by the students", "this knowledge does not concern the university, it concerns firms". Our opinion is of course different. We think that a certain level of experience can be quickly gained through lectures. Moreover, this experience is absolutely necessary when real-time applications are developed because low external quality (low dependability, high costs and delays) is unacceptable on account of the characteristics of the environments controlled by real-time applications.

6. References

[1] BENNO S., FRAILEY D., « Software Process Improvement in DSEG -1989-1995. », Texas Instruments Technical Journal, Vol. 12, No. 2, March-April, 1995, pp. 20-28.

[2] BOEHM B.W., « Verifying and Validating Software Requirements and Design Specifications », IEEE Software, January 1984, pp. 75-88.

[3] BRODMAN J. G., JOHNSON D. L., « Return on Investment (ROI) from Software Process Improvement Program as Measured by Industry », Software Process

Improvement and Practice, Wiley, Pilot Issue, August 1995, pp 35-48.

[4] BUTLER K.L., « The Economic Benefits of Software Process Improvement. », Cross Talk: The Journal of Defense Software Engineering, Vol. 8, No. 7, July, 1995, pp. 14-17.

[5] DION R., « Process Improvement and the Corporate Balance Sheet », IEEE Software, Vol. 10, No. 4, July, 1993, pp. 28-35.

[6] FLEURQUIN R., BARTHEL O., MOTET G., « Procedure Allowing Small Firms to Obtain ISO 9001 Certification », 5th Advanced Technology Workshop, Bedford, Massachussets, USA, August 7-9, 1996.

[7] GILB T., GRAHAM D., « Software Inspection », Addison-Wesley, 1993.

[8] GOLDENSON D.R., HERBSLED J.D., « After the Appraisal: A Systematic Survey of Process Improvement, its Benefits, and Factors that Influence Success », CMU/SEI-95-TR-009, ADA 300225, Pittsburgh, Pa.: Software Engineering Institute, 1995.

[9] HERBSLEB J., CARLETON A., ROZUM J., SIEGEL J., ZUBROW D., « Benefits of CMM-Based Software Process Improvement: Initial Results », CMU/SEI-94-TR-13, Software Engineering Institute, 1994.

[10] HUMPHREY W.S., SNYDER T.R., WILLIS R.R., « Software Process Improvement at Hugues Aircraft », IEEE Software, Vol. 8, No. 4, July, 1991, pp. 11-23.

[11] HUMPHREY W.S., « The Personal Process in Software Engineering », Third International Conference on the Software Process, Reston, Virginia, October 10-11, 1994, pp. 69-77.

[12] HUMPHREY W.S., « Using a Defined and Measured Personal Software Process », IEEE Software, May 1996, pp 77-88.

[13] ISO-84-02, « Quality Management and Quality Assurance - Vocabulary », ISO, 1994.

[14] JOHNSON D. L., BRODMAN J. G., « Tailoring the CMM for Small Businesses, Small Organizations, and Small Project », Software Process Newsletter, IEEE Computer Society TCSE, No. 8, Winter 1997, pp 1-5.

[15] LAPRIE J-C. (Ed.), « Dependability: Basic Concepts and Terminology », Springer-Verlag, 1992.

[16] LEVESON N.G., STOLZY J.L., « Safety Analysis Using Petri Nets », Transactions on Software Engineering, vol. SE-13, No. 3, IEEE publisher, March 1987.

[17] MOTET G., KUBEK J-M., « Dependability Problem of Ada Components Available via Information Superhighways », Proceedings of the 13th Conference on Ada Technology, Valley Forge, Pennsylvania, U.S.A., Rosenberg & Risinger Publishers, Culver City California, 13-16 March 1995, pp 8-18.

[18] MOTET G., MARPINARD A., GEFFROY J.-C., « Design of Dependable Ada Software », Prentice Hall, 1996.

[19] MOTET G., « Importance of Specification Means to Design Integrated Modular Avionics Systems », in « Embedded System Applications », Kluwer Academic Publishers, 1997.

[20] SAKAMOTO K., KISHIDA K., NAKAKOJI K., « Cultural Adaptation of the CMM: a Case Study of a Software Engineering Process Group in a Japanese Manufacturing Factory », in « Software Process », Wiley, 1996.

[21] Software Productivity Consortium, « Ada Quality and Style », SPC Building, 2214 Rock Hill Road, Herndon, Virginia, 1995.

[22] WOHLWEND H., ROSENBAUM S., « Software Improvements in an International Company », Proceedings of International Conference on Software Engineering, IEEE Computer Society Press, May 17-21, 1993.

Towards real-time systems education with PBL

Simin Nadjm-Tehrani

Dept. of Computer &
Information Science
Linköping University
S-581 83 Linköping, Sweden
(simin@ida.liu.se)

Abstract

In this report the plans for the spring term of the third year of the Information Technology *M.Sc. program in engineering at Linkping university is described. The adopted pedagogical form is inspired by the idea of Problem-Based Learning (PBL). Major ingredients in PBL are self-directed learning, and group discussions based on realistic examples. This induces a higher degree of integration among topics than is usual in traditional curricula. The spring term which is reported upon is organized around four themes of study integrating the traditional topics of concurrent programming, operating systems, real-time systems, automatic control, discrete time circuit theory, linear algebra, transform theory, and ethics. A team of several teachers from four departments of the university are involved in the implementation of this term's education.*

1   Background

Education in computer science and engineering in Sweden has been confronted with a number of challenges in the last decade. There are clear signals from the employers of computer graduates about the need for people who can face a real life problem in its entirety, and solve the problem through interaction with people from other disciplines (economists, mechanical engineers, psychologists, etc.), rather than being specialists in narrow fields or specific programming paradigms. There is also another need, becoming increasingly pronounced, which is due to the high rate of technological development in the area. That is, the call for a major goal of education being "learning to learn". A third problem, specific to the computer science and engineering educations, is the decrease in the interest of female students to choose these topics – the current levels being about 5-10% in Sweden.

In autumn 1996 a new 4.5 year educational program in computer engineering was started at Linkping university. The program aims to be an improvement over the existing programs in the above sense. The additional competence of the students in the *Information Technology* Master of Engineering program [1] is expected to arise from

- higher competence in communication and team work

- better understanding of the relationship of (traditionally) isolated topics and their integration in a real world situation

- more knowledge of humanities topics interacting with and affecting the role of the computer engineer

- the program being more attractive to female students and therefore countering the current extreme inbalance

Inspired by the *Problem-Based Learning* (PBL) pedagogical idea, a new set up totally different from the existing programs in computer education was selected.

2   PBL in an engineering setting

There are several implementations of PBL in non-technical curricula both in Sweden and elsewhere [2, 3]. We distinguish, however, between the project-based form of education common in technical education programs, and the PBL version described below. The main difference being that there is usually no "product" or result expected from the group work within PBL[1].

To describe the set up briefly, there are much fewer lectures (around half of the nominal lectures in traditional courses), and much more student group activities. Every term of study consists of a number of themes, with little or no overlap in time (i.e. no parallel courses). Each theme, however integrates a number (2 or 3) of topics normally taught in separate traditional courses.

There are regular group meetings with 6-8 students in each group and a specially educated tutor. The students' role in the group meetings is to define personal and group learning goals, given the predefined high level goals of each theme of study. The role of the tutor in this group is to act as an observer and coordinator of the group process so that all individuals achieve a high level of learning. There is no technical intervention by the tutor in the content of the discussions.

The role of the main teachers of the theme (examinators) is to define the goals and scope, the literature list, and provide a number of realistic problem scenarios (cases) to initiate the above group discussions, so that the search for and achievement of lower level learning goals is facilitated.

The whole educational program comprises 180 credit points. The parts which are covered here are the 120 points for years 1 to 3, prior to the forth year in which a specialisation profile is chosen and a final thesis is written.

The six terms designed so far cover integration of topics by teachers from different departments: mathematics, computer science, electrical engineering, physics and humanities. This report describes the design of the sixth term (the spring term in the third year) which includes real-time programming and automatic control. The author is, together with Dr. Inger Klein from the electrical engineering department, responsible for the design and administration of the team work leading to the detailed implementation.

The five earlier terms have been devoted to the themes ranging over introduction to computer science, mathematical tools, models in physics, electromagnetism, mathematical models, philosophy of science, programming, algorithms and optimization, design and construction. Moreover, there is a large project over the whole of the fifth term incorporating compiler construction and project management in in-

teraction with the economics and psychology students. Also throughout the program there is a "communication" streak in which, among others, verbal and documentational communication is learnt in the context of the main themes of study.

3   Real-time systems and automatic control

The sixth term of study is currently organized around four themes. There are some details which have to be fixed prior to the first operation of this term in spring 1998, but the overall structure is already determined. The contents of the various themes, which provide 18 credit points altogether, can be summarized as follows.

- Theme 1: Fundamentals of multi-programming and operating systems. Concurrent programming, operating systems as soft real-time systems, other operating systems topics such as memory management, file systems, security, resource management and I/O interface.

- Theme 2: Hard real-time systems with emphasis on process control applications. Mathematical models for simple dynamic systems and their time-discrete approximations, feedback, scheduling for real-time systems, program development for automatic control applications.

- Theme 3: Linear systems with feedback. Linear time-invariant systems described by linear differential equations with constant coefficients, analysis of the solutions either as functions of time or as transfer functions over complex frequency variables, Laplace tranform and linear algebra, different notions of stability, observability, controllability.

- Theme 4: Ethics in engineering. Normative ethical theories and principles, technical development and morality, ethical criteria for choice of techniques, aspects in the engineers career, case studies with ethical issues in technical settings.

The organization and the real-world cases forming the basis of the group sessions are planned as follows. There will be a number of introductory lectures about ethical theories at the beginning of the term. The students are expected to try to identify ethical issues during the first three themes in order to prepare further analysis in the last theme. Other than that, lectures

---

[1]except for formulation of learning goals – compare with the result of a project-based activity which is usually an artifact or a piece of code.

related to each theme's topics are provided during that theme, and supplemented by resource sessions where student questions are answered.

The group studies dealing with concurrency and operating systems are based upon usual scenarios and classic examples from this area (the details are not worked out yet). This will be complemented by practical individual programming using three exercises from Berkeley's Nachos educational operating system. To illustrate the techniques for deadlock avoidance we plan an exercise using the department's model train laboratory (also used in traditional courses). The exercise consists of adding an implementation of the banker's algorithm for allocation of rail segments to trains.

At the beginning of the second theme the students are introduced to a real application: a fine measurement robot for tool precision developed at a Swedish company. This application will be used in themes 2 and 3. Robot arm movements in three dimentions using three servo motors form the basis of the group discussions in the second theme. There will be a study of the stability phenomenon in a physical setting using an actual motor control exercise at the electrical engineering laboratory. This is followed by discussions around scheduling methods for real-time systems, in which the three servo processes together with I/O processes, with or without an on-line diagnosis will be studied. This exercise may even serve to illustrate the ethical issues connected wih safety of real-time systems and the "costs" for achieving safety. For the implementation exercises in this theme we are currently considering the choice between modelling and code-generation tools like Matlab or MatrixX and other scheduling and simulation environments. The ability to choose different scheduling policies and see the effect of the policy in the same example will highly influence this choice.

In the third theme transform theory, linear algebra and the theory behind automatic control will be integrated. The theme is of a theoretical nature but some exercises in Matlab are envisaged. The group discussions leading to definition of learning goals are however, expected to be focused around aspects of control fetched from the same robot application.

The fourth theme on ethics will be somewhat influenced by ethical issues appearing in safety-critical system development, computer security and connections to the operating systems theme. The choice of cases (scenarios) for group discussions is still open, but is expected to be an interesting exercise in multidicsiplinary curriculum design across two faculties.

4 Current state and future works

As mentioned above there are some detailed aspects of implementation of the sixth term left to be done. This report should therefore be seen as a description of work in progress. Once the program is implemented and run over a number of years, however, the benefits and drawbacks of the redesign in the PBL setting will certainly provide an interesting topic for further study. So far the program has had two annual intakes. Although too early to evaluate the program in its entirety, some facts can already be observed. Of the 37 and 35 students reading in the first and second year respectively, 14 and 17 are female students.

References

[1] See the web site for Swedish Council for the Renewal of Undergraduate Education, under ongoing projects:
www.hgur.se/general/projects/hems.htm.

[2] L. Wilkerson and W. Gijselaers (Eds.). Bringing Problem-Based Learning to Higher Education. Theory and Practice. San Fransisco, Jossey Bass Publishers, 1996.

[3] L.D. Distlehorst and R. Hobbs. Comparisons of Students in a Problem-Based Learning Curriculum and and a Standard Curriculum. Three Years of Data.. In *Proc. of the 3rd Education Innovation in Economics and Business Conference*, Florida, December 1996.

GHOST: A Tool for Simulation and Analysis of Real-Time Scheduling Algorithms

Fabrizio Sensini, Giorgio C. Buttazzo and Paolo Ancilotti
Scuola Superiore S. Anna, Pisa, Italy
{giorgio, paolo}@sssup.it

Abstract

This paper describes a flexible tool for the simulation and analysis of real-time applications characterized by different classes of tasks. Flexibility is achieved by allowing the user to define new scheduling algorithms directly in C language, specify the statistical characteristics of the workload, and describe the metrics and the experiments to be performed in the simulation. Tasks can be periodic or aperiodic, and can be characterized by different levels of criticality. Each task class can be handled by a separate scheduling policy, and all policies are integrated by a class scheduler, also defined by the user. Access to shared resources can be simulated by defining specific concurrency control protocols, such as Priority Inheritance, Priority Ceiling, or other user-defined protocols. The simulator has been extensively tested and used for evaluating the performance of several novel scheduling algorithms and is currently being used for research and education.

1 Introduction

GHOST (General Hard real-time Oriented Simulator Tool) is a scheduling simulator which has been designed as a tool for supporting performance studies on different scheduling strategies in a real-time environment[1]. It is part of a complete tool kit [1, 2] developed within the MORIS project [3] for supporting the design of a complex robot control application.

One could argue that simulation is not necessary in hard real-time environments, since timing constraints of critical computational activities can only be guaranteed by means of schedulability analysis. This is certainly true for all the tasks having a critical deadline, for which off-line guarantee has to be done whenever possible. In many real-world control applications, however, hard real-time activities often coexist with soft real-time and non-real-time processes, whose

arrival pattern cannot be modeled as an periodic or sporadic task, but can only be specified in terms of statistical distributions. In such systems, the schedulability analysis of the critical subset only provides a partial view of the application behavior, ignoring performance issues for non-critical activities.

This problem becomes more complex if soft real-time tasks interfere with the execution of hard tasks. Provided that hard tasks are still guaranteed off-line, the responsiveness of soft tasks strongly depends on the processor load and on the specific policy used for servicing aperiodic requests. In this case, a synthetic workload generator and a scheduling simulator are essential not only for testing the system behavior, but also for comparing the performance of different service policies and driving the design of new scheduling strategies.

At present, not much work has been done on the development of simulation tools aimed at creating and analyzing real-time scheduling algorithms. Most of the tools described in the literature [5, 8, 13, 14] have usually been developed for specific applications or environments, rather than for general purposes.

A general tool for the simulation of hard real-time systems is STRESS [4], which provides a description language for modelling the system itself and for creating task sets with predefined features. However, it focuses exclusively on tasks with hard timing requirements, without explicit support for hybrid task sets. DRTSS [10] is another general tool designed to support the simulation of distributed real-time systems, but it is not oriented to the performance analysis of scheduling algorithms. The tool developed by Lai and Callison [6] allows the user to define schedulers and concurrency control protocols, but no customization is allowed for the task model.

The most distinguishing feature of GHOST with respect to the simulators described above is the capability of handling tasks with different characteristics, such as periodic, aperiodic, hard, soft, and non-real-time, which can be defined by the user as a set of classes. The tool also allows to define new scheduling algorithms and resource allocation protocols, and supports a simple language for describing

---

[1]This work has been supported by the European Community under MORIS, project No. 20521, by CNR, project No. 96.00058.PF01, and by MURST 40%.

large and statistically generated task sets, as well as sample task sets with deterministic parameters.

2 Structure of the tool

The overall structure of the tool is shown in Figure 1. The boxes with a thick border represent the application modules, whereas those with a thin border represent the C modules (built in the simulator or provided by the user) describing the scheduling algorithms and the experiments.

The tool receives as input an ASCII file containing a description of the simulation experiment, i.e., a specification of the synthetic task set as a function of an independent variable (see Section 5). This file is processed by an interpreter, which provides the necessary data to the load generator. Based on this information, the load generator creates the task set for the simulation and produces the task instances to execute. The simulator interacts with the scheduler, which plans the next instances to be selected for execution.

When requested by the user, the simulator can optionally produce a trace of a particular simulation, for debugging, analysis or demonstration purposes. The trace file can be analyzed off-line for fixing some bug in the implementation of the scheduler or for better understanding the behavior of the scheduling algorithm under certain load conditions. The information contained in the trace file allows the user to examine the execution track, as well as system queues, user queues, and task parameters. A graphic visualization tool is also provided to perform such an analysis. Particular events (e.g., a secondary deadline) and variables (e.g., dynamic server capacities) can also be associated with the tasks or the system to be displayed along with the trace. Figure 2 shows an example of trace produced by the simulator.

The output generator module is invoked every time a measurement has to be done on some particular event. This module interacts with a user-defined output specification module, collects its data, extracts the needed statistical values and stores them in the output file (see Section 6).

3 The Machine Model

GHOST has been designed to perform simulation and analysis of real-time task sets running on a uniprocessor machine. At the lowest level, called the *CPU level*, the simulator provides a machine model, which is used to build a virtual real-time operating system. At this level, GHOST performs the execution of a pseudo-code and implements a priority based interrupt mechanism which allows time management. The pseudo-code "executed" by the virtual processor cannot perform any significant operation, aside from consuming time and invoking kernel primitives for accessing shared resources. Each pseudo-instruction causes the

simulator to evaluate a time quantity according to a distribution pattern and consume such a quantity. The particular distribution can be defined by the user.

To study the effects of system overhead on the performance of various scheduling algorithms, the notion of time has been provided at two different resolutions: a major tick and a minor tick, whose ratio can be defined by the user. The major tick defines the unit of time for expressing all tasks' timing parameters, and is the basis for the interrupt mechanism and for the timer routine which periodically invokes the scheduler. The minor tick represents the time resolution and it is the smallest quantity that can be executed by the simulator. To increase flexibility, the simulator can work in a time-driven or an event-driven fashion.

At the next level (the *Kernel level*), the simulator provides the notion of "task" and supports the typical primitives for task management, such as creation, termination, and context switch. It also supports different classes of tasks and a protocol template for accessing shared resources (the latter must be completely specified by the user, in order to implement a specific resource access protocol). A task class denotes a set of tasks with the same kind of timing constraints and generation mechanism. For example, the user may define hard periodic and soft aperiodic tasks as two different classes, or define a single aperiodic task class for aperiodic specific studies. By defining different task classes, the user can customize the real-time machine to specific application requirements.

4 The scheduler

The user-defined scheduler is inserted above the kernel layer. It is structured as a set of C functions, each of which is called upon the occurrence of specific events, such as a new task arrival, a task completion, a deadline miss, and so on. New functions can be associated with each event, so that new algorithms can easily be created and modified by the user.

To increase the flexibility of the simulator, the scheduling algorithm is divided into two levels: a set of *task schedulers*, each of which selects a task for execution within a specific task class, and a *class scheduler*, which selects one of the given classes. A large number of schedulers are already provided by the simulator and new ones can easily be created by the user. A block diagram of the simulator is illustrated in Figure 3.

For example, if two classes of tasks are defined by the user (e.g., hard periodic and soft aperiodic), a Sporadic Server could be implemented as a class scheduler, whereas Rate Monotonic and First Come First Served could be specified as task schedulers for periodic and aperiodic tasks respectively. Although the two-level scheduler allows great flexibility, it can easily be replaced by a single general scheduling

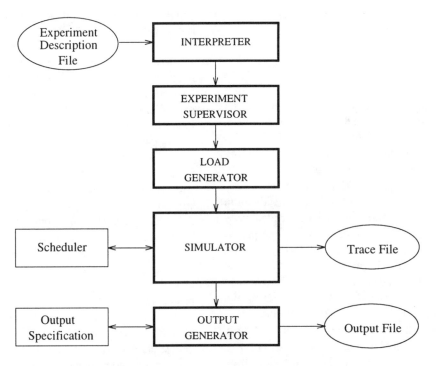

Figure 1. Overall structure of the tool.

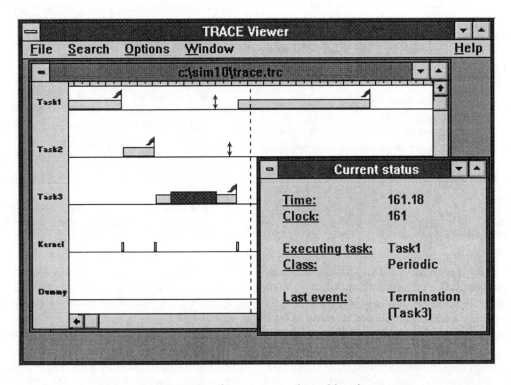

Figure 2. Example of output produced by the tracer.

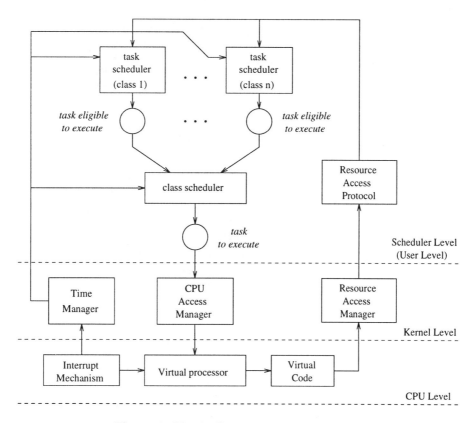

Figure 3. Block diagram of the simulator.

manager.

To describe a resource access protocol the user must provide a C function (Resource Access Manager) for each existing task class. At each resource request or release, the appropriate class resource manager is invoked. Within these functions, the user can describe his own protocol using a monitor-like semantics.

The development of a scheduling algorithm is extensively supported by the GHOST library, which provides a complete set of functions for system state inquiry and setting, queue management, and scheduling and resource management (see Table 1).

A large number of scheduling strategies have been implemented in GHOST and can be used or modified according to the user's needs. Figure 4 shows the Rate Monotonic algorithm as can be implemented in GHOST.

Each task scheduler has to be defined as a C function with two input parameters, which represent the event to be handled and the task which the event refers to. In this example, a single class is defined (PERIODIC) and the function Psched is declared as a scheduler for it. A task queue is associated with a newly created class and the queue discipline is set to the predefined RM_PRIO discipline, which assigns each task a priority proportional to the inverse of its period. To introduce user-defined disciplines a specific function has

to be provided which realizes a different priority mapping. The pointer to this function has to be linked to the class queue by the UserQueDis() primitive.

Three events are handled by the Psched scheduler: job arrival, job completion, and deadline miss. At the arrival time, the new job t is inserted into the ready queue and the highest priority task is scheduled[2].

At completion time, the task is removed from the ready queue and the highest priority task is scheduled. Finally, if a deadline is missed the SimException primitive stops the simulation and outputs the specified error message.

5 The load generator

The experiment description file parsed by the interpreter is written in a C-like language, designed to describe deterministic as well as statistical task sets. In order to easily describe the statistical properties of a task set, the language supports array operations and provides the most common statistical distribution functions which may also operate on arrays. When defining a task set, arrays of tasks can be created and associated with statistically described variables for the task parameters the user chooses.

---

[2]A dummy task is always present in each queue, so that a queue can never be empty.

function	description
Time()	returns the current time in minor ticks
Clock()	returns the current time in major ticks
ExeTask()	returns the currently executing task
Class(task)	returns the class of a task
Period(task)	returns the period of a task
Deadline(task)	returns the deadline of a task
SysQueue(class)	returns the queue associated with a class
TaskInsert(task, queue)	inserts a task in a queue
TaskExtract(task, queue)	extracts a task from a queue
FirstTask(queue)	returns the first task of a queue
SetTaskPrio(task, p)	sets the priority of a task
SetQueDis(queue, ptype)	sets the queue discipline
TaskSchedule(task, class)	selects a task from a class
ClassSchedule(class)	selects a class for execution
Lock(res, task)	locks a resource to a task
Unlock(res)	unlocks a resource from a task

Table 1. A selection of functions available in GHOST.

The experiment description file specifies the range and the step of increment for the variable to be changed during a simulation experiment. Another parameter associated with this variable specifies the number of simulations to be performed for each value of it. This is necessary for reducing simulation "noise", that is, shrinking the confidence intervals obtained on the resulting outputs. The file also contains declarations of the task classes and a description of the task set.

Different task sets can be created for different simulations associated with the same value. This can be done by describing auxiliary task parameters as functions of the independent variable. Such a dependency can be introduced anywhere in the description of the tasks. For instance, task periods can be expressed as random variables uniformly distributed around the value of the experiment variable, with a given tolerance. A task class declaration implies the definition of common timing properties, such as the level of criticality, and generation patterns. Within a specific class, tasks can be generated periodically or aperiodically, in a limited number of instances, if desired.

Once task classes are defined, a specific task set has to be declared. Notice that each task is considered as a sequence of instances which execute the same pseudo-code. To define a task, the user has to specify the task class it belongs to, the pseudo-code to execute and a set of class specific attributes (such as the period for periodic tasks). In addition, a set of user values can be associated to tasks for specific applications. For instance, the user might want to assign tasks importance values or jitter constraints to investigate new scheduling policies.

The pseudo-code is a list of instructions which specify the amount of time required for the execution. Each instruction provides a statistical description of the amount of time to consume, along with the parameters needed by the statistical description itself. For example, the pseudo-instruction $unif(alpha)$ requires a time consumption uniformly distributed in the range $[0, 2 * alpha]$. For each task instance, the simulator evaluates at run time the actual time to consume according to the statistical description provided by the user. If the generation pattern of the task is aperiodic, a statistical description of the interarrival time has to be provided, which has the same form of the pseudo-code description.

The simulation description language reserves a set of predefined variable identifiers for basic system settings. By means of an assignment statement on any of these variables, the user can set the ratio between the major and the minor tick, introduce default time consumption for the main system primitives (to take overhead into account), or specify some parameters to be passed to the scheduler (as for instance the server period).

Figure 5 shows a typical task set declaration (words in upper case represent language keywords). In this example, 50 aperiodic tasks are created with an average workload rho. Each task has a critical section on a common resource, with a deterministic duration, and a non-critical code whose execution time is modeled as a random variable with a uniform distribution. The interarrival time for each task is given by the sum of a minimum interarrival time and a random time with an exponential distribution. Each task is assigned a

```
#include "ghost.h"

void SchedInit() {

        /* Creates the PERIODIC class with Psched as a scheduler */
        ClassCreate(PERIODIC, Psched);
        SetQueDis(SysQueue(PERIODIC), RM_PRIO);
}

void Psched(EVENT_T ev, TASK t) {

        switch (ev) {
                case ARRIVAL:
                        TaskInsert(t, SysQueue(PERIODIC));
                        t = FirstTask(SysQueue(PERIODIC));
                        TaskSchedule(t, PERIODIC);
                        break;

                case END:
                        TaskExtract(t, SysQueue(PERIODIC));
                        t = FirstTask(SysQueue(PERIODIC));
                        TaskSchedule(t, PERIODIC);
                        break;

                case DEADLINE:
                        SimException("Deadline miss!!");
        }
}
```

Figure 4. The Rate Monotonic Algorithm.

deadline 50 times longer than its average execution time.

The function $unif(n)$ returns a random number uniformly distributed in $[0, 2n]$, whereas the function $pois(a, b)$ provides a random variable with exponential distribution with average a and upper bound b. Arithmetic operators and functions are automatically extended to deal with arrays. Expressions like $[n]v$ produce an array of n elements of value v. For example, the avg_exec_time variable is an array of variables uniformly distributed between 500 and 1500 minor ticks. The interarrival times are evaluated to obtain the desired workload rho. The det function (standing for 'deterministic') simply returns its argument, and it has been introduced just to improve readability.

6 The output specification module

Given the variety of scheduling algorithms proposed in the literature and the different performance metrics that could be used to evaluate the performance of a system, any predefined approach for producing simulation results would be too restrictive. To cope with this need, GHOST provides a set of data structures for recording statistical values of parameters which the user wishes to monitor during simulation. A related set of C functions is then used to pass such results to the output generation module.

Figure 6 shows how to monitor the maximum response time and the average queue length for a single class of tasks. The EVENT_REC type is used to declare variables for recording quantities generated at particular events (e.g., a response time, generated at task completion), whereas the TIME_REC type is used for monitoring quantities that are functions of time (e.g., the length of a queue or an aperiodic server capacity). Once declared, a recording variable must be initialized to specify a label to reference the variable in the output file and the desired statistical parameters to be computed on such a variable (minimum, maximum, average, or standard deviation).

```
EXPERIMENT VARIABLE rho:
        RANGE [0.2,0.8], STEP 0.1, REPEAT 100

CLASS sporadic = SOFT, APERIODIC;
SEMAPHORE sem;

avg_exec_time = 500 + UNIF([50]500);
task_load = rho / 50;
avg_inter_time = avg_exec_time / task_load;

sporadic[50] {
        CRITICAL sem {
                DET(avg_exec_time / 2);
        }
        UNIF(avg_exec_time / 2);
}

INTERARRIVAL_TIME {
        DET(avg_inter_time / 2);
        EXP(avg_inter_time / 2, avg_inter_time * 20);
}

DEADLINE_AT avg_exec_tim * 50;
```

Figure 5. Example of task set declaration.

To simplify the specification of the output, a set of pre-defined general purpose measurement modules is provided for evaluating the mean aperiodic completion time, the global system overhead, the length of the system predefined queues, and so on.

For example, the function EventRec(&resp_time, "rtime", MAX_R) associates the label rtime to the variable resp_time and causes the output generation module to compute the maximum among the values of the variable. The primitive Monitor(event, userfunc) binds a user-defined function to a runtime event. In particular, function TestTaskArr() causes the output generation module to increment the queue_len variable at each task arrival. Similarly, function TestTaskEnd() acts on the resp_time and queue_len variables.

7   Conclusions

In this paper we presented the structure of GHOST, a flexible simulator tool for testing the performance of various scheduling algorithms in a real-time environment.

As a future work, the tool will be extended to simulate multiprocessor and distributed computing environments. In doing so, a more general framework must be introduced, and far more complex issues are involved, as concerns on time synchronization, task communication and so on. But once the general system model is defined, the implementation should easily follow. Also the experiment description interpreter is to be enhanced, to produce different kinds of experiments.

Other improvements will be oriented to increase efficiency and simulation speed. This is a fundamental concern, provided that, for research studies upon the performance of scheduling algorithms, several simulations are necessary to achieve acceptable results on large and statistically defined task sets (which means significant and virtually noise-free outputs).

References

[1] P. Ancilotti, G.C. Buttazzo, M. Di Natale, M. Spuri, "A Development Environment for Real-Time Applications", *The Journal of Software Engineering and Knowledge Engineering*, pp. 91–99, September 1996.

```
#include "ghost.h"

EVENT_REC resp_time;        /* response time */
TIME_REC queue_len;         /* queue length */

void TestTaskArr() {
        AddTimeRec(&queue_len, 1);
}

void TestTaskEnd(TASK t) {
        UpdEventRec(&resp_time, Time() - Arrival(t));
        AddTimeRec(&queue_len, -1);
}

void TestInit() {
        /* Initialize recording data structures */
        EventRec(&resp_time, "rtime", MAX_R);
        TimeRec(&queue_len, "qlen", AVG_R);
        Monitor(ARRIVAL, TestTaskArr);
        Monitor(END, TestTaskEnd);
}
```

Figure 6. Sample output specification module for RM scheduling algorithm.

[2] P. Ancilotti, G.C. Buttazzo, M. Di Natale, M. Bizzarri, "A Flexible Tool Kit for the Development of Real-Time Applications", *Proc. of the IEEE Real-time Technology and Application Symposium*, Brookline, pp. 260–262, June 1996.

[3] P. Ancilotti, G. Buttazzo, M. Di Natale, M. Bizzarri, "The MORIS Control System", *Proc. of the 8th IEEE Euromicro Workshop on Real-Time Systems*, L'Aquila, Italy, pp. 77–82, June 1996.

[4] N. C. Audsley, A. Burns, M. F. Richardson and A. J. Wellings, "STRESS: a simulator for hard real-time systems." *Software Practice and Experience*, 24(6), pp. 543–564, June 1994.

[5] T.-W. Kuo and A. K. Mok, "SSP: A Semantics-based Protocol For Real-time Data Access", *Proc. of the IEEE Real-Time Systems Symposium*, Raleigh-Durham, pp. 76–86, December 1993.

[6] C. Lai and R. Callison, "A Framework for Simulation of Concurrency Control Policy in Real-time systems", *Proc. of the IEEE Real-time Technology and Application Symposium*, Brookline, pp. 91–99, June 1996.

[7] J.P. Lehoczky and S. Ramos-Thuel, "An Optimal Algorithm for Scheduling Soft-Aperiodic Tasks in Fixed-Priority Preemptive Systems," *Proc. of Real-Time Systems Symposium*, 1992, pp. 110–123.

[8] X. Song, "Data Temporal Consistency in Hard Real-Time Systems", Ph.D. Dissertation, University of Illinois at Urbana-Champaign, 1992.

[9] B. Sprunt, L. Sha, and J.P. Lehoczky, "Aperiodic Task Scheduling for Hard-Real-Time Systems," *The Journal of Real-Time Systems* 1, 1989, pp. 27–60.

[10] M. F. Storch and J.W.S. Liu, "DRTSS: A Simulation Framework for Complex Real-Time Systems", *Proc. of the IEEE Real-Time Technology and Applications Symposium*, Brookline, pp. 160–169, June 1996.

[11] J.K. Strosnider, J.P. Lehoczky, and L. Sha, "The Deferrable Server Algorithm for Enhanced Aperiodic Responsiveness in Hard Real-Time Environments", *IEEE Transactions on Computers*, 44(1), January 1995.

[12] T.S. Tia, J.W.S. Liu, and M. Shankar, "Algorithms and Optimality of Scheduling Aperiodic Requests in Fixed-Priority Preemptive Systems", *The Journal of Real-Time Systems*, 1995.

[13] H. Tokuda and M. Kotera, "A Real-Time Tool Set for the ARTS Kernel," *Proc. of the IEEE Real-Time Systems Symposium*, 1988.

[14] H. Tokuda, T. Nakajima, and P. Rao, "Real-Time Mach: Towards a Predictable Real-Time System," *Proc. Usenix Mach Workshop*, October 1990.

Variations on a Real-Time Software Design Course using ObjecTime

Terry Shepard, Jean Dolbec and Colin Wortley
Department of Electrical and Computer Engineering
Royal Military College of Canada
Station Forces, PO Box 17000, Kingston, Ontario, K7K 3B4, Canada
{shepard, wortley, dolbec-j}@rmc.ca

Abstract

The Royal Military College of Canada (RMC) has offered a real-time software design course for 4 years as part of its software engineering option in Computer Engineering. The course is intended to make the students appreciate why the techniques taught are important, and to understand the importance and difficulty of seamlessness, from requirements to target. For the last 3 years, the course has been based on the Real-Time Object-Oriented Methodology (ROOM) [1] and the ObjecTime toolset that is based on ROOM [2]. Reasons for that choice are given in [3]. This year, variations have been introduced in about one-third of the course. This paper examines the variations and discusses the reasons for them. It also illustrates the problems of deciding what to teach in a course on real-time software design, as the authors of the present paper work closely together, but nonetheless teach variations of the course, although all support the main concepts underlying the course.

1. Introduction

The variations that are possible in a course on real-time software design are enormous. In this paper, we discuss the variations we have introduced within the past year in the undergraduate real-time systems design course at RMC. Our objective in the course is to give the students an understanding of how to approach real-time software design by giving them an opportunity to do some design in the course, using techniques that are taught in the course. The course is 14 weeks long, with 3 hours of lecture and 2 hours of lab time per week, and is given in both English and French. It is also taken by graduate students as partial fulfilment for a graduate course in software design. There is clearly a need for a greater consensus as to what the most important aspects are for a single course in this area, but that consensus has not yet been reached. Our contribution is toward a better understanding of the issues involved in reaching this consensus. One point that is clear to all of us is the importance of picking a coherent approach to design and

using it as the basis for the course. Our choice of ROOM [1], as described in [3], can be justified quite strongly, but it is not the only possible choice. There are advantages to the students in being exposed to a variety of design notations and implementation environments. Our decision has been to focus on a single approach, to give the students a solid point of reference for other approaches they may see after graduation, and also because there is not time to consider alternatives in depth. The choice of ROOM has been complemented with the use of the ObjecTime toolset [2], which implements the ROOM notation and design philosophy. This paper presents a discussion of the variations that we have introduced in the two parallel versions of this undergraduate course, in English and French respectively. It also identifies the rational for such variations and outlines the benefits of each approach.

By way of background, we outline the preparation the students have prior to taking this course, and the knowledge that faculty members teaching the course must possess. The software option in the RMC computer engineering curriculum is described in [4]. It includes about 8 courses that prepare the students to do software development. The course described in this paper is in the final term of the fourth and last year of the program. By the time the students take it, they know how to program in several languages (currently including Ada and C++), they have an understanding of how operating systems work internally, and they have been exposed to object-oriented analysis and design, and to a set of work products as part of a software engineering process. Anyone teaching this course must have at least this background, and also must be familiar with different approaches to real-time software design, including the one taught in the course.

2. 1995/96 version of the course

The starting point for the variations was the 1995/96 version of the course:

i.   Introduction to real-time systems, review of operating systems concepts, and overview of x86 architecture in order to conduct the context switching lab (2 weeks);

ii.   Real-Time Structured Analysis and Design (RTSAD) ([5],[6]) (2 weeks);

iii.   ROOM methodology and ObjecTime toolset (5 weeks);

iv.   Software Cost Reduction (SCR) notation developed at the Naval Research Laboratory for precise, reviewable specification of software requirements [7], and an alarm clock example [8] (3 weeks); and

v.   Schedulability issues, and Rate Monotonic Analysis in particular (2 weeks) . This section is important, not least because ObjecTime provides essentially no support for timing and schedulability analysis, although there is some recent research that may eventually lead to such support.

3. Student concerns

Issues raised by some students who took this version of the course included:

i.   The use of the tutorial developed for a four day short course on ROOM and ObjecTime [9], was not the ideal approach for a semester based course. It offers a step by step sequence of activities, with little room for application of the ideas. In a short course, this is appropriate, since students in such a course bring their applications with them, and take away their new knowledge to apply in their regular jobs.

ii.   Following the tutorial, the students immediately began work on a relatively big problem. They would have preferred a set of smaller and more manageable problems to start. The alarm clock problem [8], although an interesting exercise in creating a design from a specification, did not capture the imagination of some students. They tended to want to ignore the details of the specification, and assume that they could do a design that suited their concept of how an alarm clock should work. They also wanted to work on the design of a more realistic real-time system, rather than such a self-contained and apparently simple device.

iii.   Some students failed to see the benefit of using ObjecTime/ROOM to develop real-time systems, or any system. A significant issue raised was that no implementation was completed all the way to a target. Students were unable to make the mental link to their earlier experience with implementation by writing the code themselves, and so were frustrated that they could not develop actual working systems.

iv.   For some students, the two weeks spent learning x86

assembler and architecture was too short and distracted from context switching issues.

4. Variations in 1996/97

The two main variations were between the course as taught in English, and the course as taught in French. We will refer to them as versions 1 and 2, respectively. The main differences in approach for 1996/97 were:

The major choice was between emphasizing high level design issues versus a deeper understanding of the complexity inherent in how real-time software interacts with its environment. In version 1 of the course, the emphasis was put on the transition from requirements to design, while in version 2, it was on the transition from design to implementation.

In version 1 of the course, this meant spending more time on RTSAD, and presenting the SCR methodology. In version 2 of the course, more time was spent on the concepts related to completing the implementation of real-time systems designs, and discussing issues related to real-time kernels, memory management, communication, and synchronization.

In the laboratory (which consisted of 16 Sun Sparcstations 4 and 5 with the minimum 32 MB RAM needed to run ObjecTime) , the main differences are as follows:

In version 1 of the course, a number of adjustments were made to respond to the issues raised by the students, but the basic content was relatively unchanged. The alarm clock example was used, as it has been for the past 3 years. It requires the students to read and understand a formal specification for the behaviour of an alarm clock [8], written using the SCR notation [7]. They then provide a high level design using the ObjecTime tool, derived from the requirements specification.

In version 2 of the course, the changes were more extensive. The students had two projects. For each project, a high level design, a low level design, and an implementation on the target environment using the ObjecTime toolset were generated.   In the first project, the students used a specification developed using the Booch methodology [10]. In the second project, they had to develop the specification as they developed their designs. The latter approach more closely resembles current industrial practice, although it is supported in the course by a more coherent methodology and toolset than is often the case in industry.

More detailed descriptions of the changes in the 1996/97 versions of the course follow.

4.1. Version 1 of the Course

First, more emphasis was placed on system design decisions and the unique properties and requirements of embedded systems. Only one week of class time (instead of two weeks) was spent on RTSAD, to review Data Flow Diagrams (DFDs), and to add the concept of Control Flow Diagrams (CFDs) [5][6]. This provided the students with a context in which to learn and evaluate the ROOM methodology. The two week laboratory which covered the use of DFDs and CFDs was replaced by an introductory tutorial in ObjecTime using a simple example. At the same time, material covered in class showed how to expand upon these simple concepts and apply them to the more realistic design example used throughout the course text [1] and in the next six weeks in the lab. Class time was also used to discuss and justify the design decisions and approach used in the textbook design example.

The presentation of the material in the tutorial [9] was modified to emphasize the design approach and the reasons behind the design decisions that are made in the tutorial.

In addition to presenting the SCR methodology as before, the alarm clock example was modified by including a discussion on some of the system design decisions that had to be made and how the partitioning of the system into hardware and software drives the system and software design. As well, there was discussion of the extent to which an SCR style specification is or is not really independent of design, and by extension, of whether any requirements specification can really completely avoid imposing some design decisions.

4.2. Version 2 of the Course

In version 2 of the course for 1996/97, the changes were more extensive. The Motorola 68000 and its assembler were used for the context switching lab. The students are already familiar with 68000 assembler. Less than one hour was spent on RTSAD. The students are already familiar with DFDs and state transition diagrams, so only CFDs [5][6] needed to be discussed in detail.

ROOM was introduced much earlier in the term. In addition, the concepts and the tools (ObjecTime implementation mechanisms) required to implement real-time systems from a design onto a target were presented. In particular, this decision prompted the need to discuss the issue of the RPL to C++ transition that is normally part of all actual implementations on a target with ObjecTime. RPL (Rapid Prototyping Language) is a Smalltalk like language that is used at early stages of the design process in ObjecTime because less effort is needed to code in RPL than in C++. The students are tempted to want to code in C++ directly from the beginning, so it is important to make them understand that this is not good practice in a large project, primarily because a lot of early code tends to be thrown away, so the less effort put into it, the better. On the other hand, there is a trade-off, because the cost of conversion from RPL to C++ can be significant.

New material was added to extend what the students had learned from an operating system course taken earlier. The new material dealt primarily with real-time operating systems concepts, but it included other issues of implementation on a target platform. Topics covered included real-time kernels, real-time memory management, real-time process communication and synchronisation, and real-time programming languages.

To address the new direction taken by the course, a major re-writing of the labs was required as follows:

Lab 1: Context switching lab on the 68000. Students had to build a mini real-time kernel in its entirety.

Lab 2: Introduction to ObjecTime - RPL. In this lab the students completed the OT RPL tutorial which is excellent for covering some of the basics. It was complemented by the design of control software in RPL for a production line.

Lab 3: Introduction to ObjecTime - C++. In this lab, the students completed an implementation on a target platform using the control software generated as part of Lab 2 in C++. This lab presented the principles and philosophy related to implementing a C++ model from a RPL model;

Lab 4: Advanced concepts in C++ with ObjecTime. This lab introduced the students to the concepts of threads in C++ and also required the use of ObjecTime timing services and the mechanisms involved in sending and retrieving C++ data objects from ObjecTime messages.

Lab 5: This lab demonstrated the benefits of using ObjecTime. The students were required to design and implement a stopwatch using an analysis conducted in a previous course using the Booch methodology. In the previous course, creation of an executive object was needed to create the illusion of concurrency. In the ObjecTime version, the need for the executive object was replaced by the Micro Run Time System (RTS) and real concurrency was established by the use of threads supported by the Micro RTS.

Lab 6: In this lab, the students were required to design and implement on a target platform a miniature version of a complete real time avionics system: a Ground Collision Avoidance System (GCAS). The system requires the use of threads and timing services. The use of timing services is extremely important in this lab as data from the various avionics sensors needs to be retrieved at specific and varying time intervals.

5. Discussion

As stated above, the major difference between the two versions of the course comes from the choice of putting the emphasis on the transition from requirements to design or from design to implementation. The choice of approach results in several differences which are discussed in the following.

5.1. Context Switching Lab

In its original version, the context switching lab required that the students become familiar with basic x86 architecture and assembly language and modify a pre-existing assembly code for a mini kernel. The 68000 version of the lab required that the students build a real-time mini kernel from scratch and allowed the students to better concentrate on the issues of context switching. Because the students did not have to learn a new assembler and architecture, they could spend more time concentrating on context switching issues. However, this approach did not give them the opportunity to learn the x86 architecture and assembler nor could they experiment with a more powerful debugger (CodeView) as it applies to debugging real-time systems.

5.2. The Short Course Tutorial

When supplemented by additional discussion on the design decisions that are reflected in the tutorial [9], it is a good introduction to the issues of going from requirements to design. However, it is not a good starting point for building the knowledge needed to complete an implementation on a target platform and was therefore not used in the French version of the course.

5.3. Introducing ROOM Earlier

In version 2 of the course, it was necessary to introduce ROOM as early as possible to have time to deal with implementation issues. This decision took advantage of the fact that the students knew C++, state transition diagrams, and the OO concept. Even though the ObjecTime toolset is powerful and complex, it was felt that the students did not need to be sheltered from it. To get the full benefit of working with ObjecTime, they should be exposed to its full functionality.

Teaching ObjecTime early in the semester, and giving students small problems is a good way to deal with the complexities of the design of real-time systems and of ObjecTime as students get more and more involved with their lab assignments.

In version 1 of the course, ROOM was introduced one week earlier as a result of reducing the time spent on RTSAD.

5.4. Implementation on a Target

Both versions of the course are based on the study of five characteristics that are common to real-time systems: timeliness, reactivity, distribution, concurrency and dynamic internal structure [1]. ObjecTime is used to gain insight into these characteristics. While it is desirable to learn as much as possible about such a powerful tool as ObjecTime, care must be taken to maintain the focus on these five characteristics. One major decision is how long to stay with RPL, and if and when to move to C++. Conversion to C++ is required if a target implementation is to be realized.

In version 1 of the course, the use of C++ as part of ObjecTime was not covered. This allowed more time for detailed discussion of the transition from requirements to design, and of system design issues as they affect the cost and efficiency of the final design. The students were still able to execute a model in the ObjecTime simulation environment, using RPL, and therefore were exposed to some of the advantages of the ROOM methodology and of using the ObjecTime tool.

In version 2 of the course the emphasis was put on how the five characteristics impact design decisions and what are the resulting effects on the implementation and execution environment. By taking the design to an implementation, the students were able to get experience with threads and concurrency issues, and with the difficulty of designing to meet timing constraints. With this approach the students also had the satisfaction of implementing complete real-time systems.

5.5. Choice of Final Project

As mentioned before, to support the approach taken by version 1, the final project consisted of an analysis of the SCR requirements for an alarm clock [8] and the modelling in ObjecTime of a design to meet such requirements. The alarm clock example was shown to require several major design decisions which had to be made very early. Use of the ObjecTime tool greatly enhances the student's ability to model, understand, and test these early design decisions in an effective manner. Use of the alarm clock example also has the added benefit of exposing the students to the SCR requirements specification methodology, and to the potential limitations of that technique. These limitations could be reduced by using the SCRtool produced by NRL [11], but the problem of finding time for the students to learn how to use the SCRtool will be hard to solve. In the current version of the course, a careful analysis by hand of the requirements as given in [8] shows that they are incomplete, so some properties of the alarm clock's final operation become dependent on design decisions. Use of the alarm clock example also makes the students realize that what, on the surface, appears to be a self-contained and simple device is anything but when it comes to actually designing and implementing the control software. Emphasis is also put on the issues of minimizing overall system cost. In particular, [8] makes no mention of the hardware that will be used to support the software being designed, so the students are exposed to the effects that hardware design decisions have on the software process. Issues such as whether buttons should cause interrupts or should be polled, and how the hardware should supply the timing signal needed to make the alarm clock work, and the effect such issues have on cost, are discussed in version 1 of the course.

From the perspective of version 2 of the course, the alarm clock did not constitute a problem that would properly bring out many of the issues related to concurrency and timeliness. As a result, a new project was needed to better address these issues. To fulfill this requirement, a project was developed which involved the design and implementation of a miniature version of an aircraft Ground Collision Avoidance System (GCAS) avionics system. The GCAS is a hard real-time system which requires concurrency and prioritization in order to meet its deadlines. The GCAS lab provided insight into designing a system that performs specific tasks at given time intervals, and that also must respond to asynchronous events. It also demonstrated the difficulty of modelling components that are external to the design. There are a number of other avionics systems that GCAS has to interact with. In the real GCAS, the data produced by these systems is tightly coupled, in the sense that aircraft attitude, altitude, speed, heading, acceleration and so on are all interdependent, even though the data representing them may come from different systems. It was necessary to implement a simple simulated flight profile to allow the students to run their designs.

6. Conclusion

In our view, the changes made for 96/97 have resulted in two improved versions of the course. There is obviously debate amongst us as to which of the two versions of the course is most appropriate. We do not have a way of settling the debate, other than to wait to see what the future brings. In both courses, the students acquired a deeper understanding of issues related to the design of real-time systems, as well as

a greater understanding of the ObjecTime environment. We have taken care to steer the students around the complexities of ObjecTime, and to focus on the important issues.

It is difficult to make an assessment of the effect of the two versions of the course on the two groups of students, each taking one of the versions. Both groups seem satisfied with the version they took, but that is to be expected, since none of the students have other points of reference from which to judge whether something is missing, or to judge what is most important. If the professors are having difficulty with such judgements, the students should be having even more difficulty!

There can be a tendency on the part of the students to believe that there is one correct approach to a design. In both version of the course, the students were required to give a brief presentation of their project designs. This exercise exposed the students to various solutions and made them realize that there is more than one sound design that solves a given problem. It also allowed us to critique their different designs.

A significant issue is whether the students gain a sufficient appreciation of the limitations of older approaches to real-time software design, and specifically of the issue of "phase discontinuity" as emphasized in the course text [1]. There is some doubt that they do, both in version 2 of the course, and to a lesser extent in version 1 (where more time is spent on RTSAD). We all agree that RTSAD will eventually be entirely removed from the course.

In version 2 of the course, it was advantageous to build directly on a previous course in object-oriented techniques, taught by the same instructor to the same students, which used the Booch approach to analysis and design, and C++ for implementation. The instructor for version 1 of the course did not teach the corresponding previous course to the students taking version 1, and the material covered was different enough to mean that direct use of it was not feasible. For instance, in version 2, virtually no time was spent on state transition diagrams or C++, as they had been thoroughly covered in the earlier course. This was not so clearly true for the students in version 1. Also, drawing directly on some of the lab work done in the previous course allowed the students in version 2 to tackle more ambitious lab projects, and allowed them to see more clearly the benefits of ObjecTime.

For the labs that were given, a good understanding of C was all that was required. C++ is not essential unless the students have to modify the code generated by ObjecTime. On the other hand, modifying the generated code is part of the reality of real-time system construction, even with ObjecTime. Ideally, the students would modify one of their designs, and then be able to do design recovery from modified code. This may be difficult, depending on the nature of the modifications, and the extent to which they are expressible in ObjecTime. On the other hand, it is an objective worth attaining, since it is important for the students to understand the importance of the integrity of a design, and to learn approaches to maintaining integrity.

This course is part of a six course set of courses in the third and fourth years of a four year program in computer engineering at RMC, taken by the students who follow the software option. Three of the courses are taken by all computer engineering students; this course is one of the remaining three courses that constitute the software option. The program in its entirety is a good candidate, with a bit more software content, to be accredited as a software engineering undergraduate program. The present course makes an important contribution to this possibility.

Changing views of what is important in the software world, combined with our experiences with this course, and with other courses in the set, plus the possibility of adding a seventh course, will undoubtedly result in further changes to the whole program. We would ideally like to have objective evaluations of the different approaches to this course, and to the whole program, preferably via statistically valid studies, but RMC is too small to permit this, even if all our students actually had the opportunity to do real-time software design immediately after graduation. Many of them eventually do related things, but later in their careers.

7. References

[1] Bran Selic, Garth Gullekson and Paul Ward, Real-Time Object-Oriented Modelling, J. Wiley, 1994

[2] ObjecTime and MicroRTS manuals, ObjecTime, Kanata, Ontario, 1997

[3] Terry Shepard, Colin Wortley, and Bran Selic, "Using ObjecTime to Teach Real-Time Software in the Undergraduate Curriculum", Real-Time Systems Education, Ed. J. Zalewski, IEEE Computer Society Press, 1996, pp. 26-35

[4] Terry Shepard, "Software Engineering in an Undergraduate Computer Engineering Program", Proceedings of the 7th SEI Conference on Software Engineering Education, San Antonio, TX, 5-7 January 1994, pp. 23-34

[5] Derek J. Hatley, and Pirbhai, I.A., Strategies for Real-Time System Specification, Dorset House, 1987

[6] Paul T. Ward, and Mellor, S.J., Structured Development for Real-Time Systems, Volumes 1, 2 & 3, Yourdon Press, 1985

[7] Katherine L. Heninger, "Specifying Software Requirements for Complex Systems: New Techniques and Their Application", IEEE Transactions on Software Engineering, v. 6, n. 1, Jan 1980, pp. 2-13

[8] Peter Matelski and James McKim, "Alarm Clock Requirements", January 11 1988, Queen's University internal teaching note.

[9] Paul T. Ward, "ObjecTime Curriculum: New User Workshop: Basic Modelling", Paul Ward Associates, New York City, NY, 1995

[10] Grady Booch Object-Oriented Analysis and Design with Applications, 2nd Edition, Benjamin/Cummings, 1994

[11] SCRtool, Naval Research Laboratories, Washington, DC, USA (contact: Connie Heitmeyer, heitmeye@itd.nrl.navy.mil)

Chapter 3

Real-Time Projects and Labs

Teaching Simple Sound Synthesis:
Real-Time, Numeric and Symbolic Computation

Kenneth H. Jacker
Computer Science Department
Appalachian State University
Boone, NC 28608 USA
khj@cs.appstate.edu

Abstract

*The paper begins with a short description of equipment available to students in the Department's real-time course. This is followed by an overview of specific software packages for data and function visualization, numeric calculation, and symbolic manipulation. After a discussion of the structure of a typical data acquisition application and functions available within the **mr** real-time library, the paper concludes with details of a series of four "sound synthesis" labs.*

1 Introduction

The process of generating analog voltages from discrete digital samples [20, 3] is one of many topics covered in the Department's *Real-Time Systems (CS4620)* course [13]. Although the first synthesis lab only uses an oscilloscope to verify signals generated by a digital-to-analog converter (DAC), later labs provide audible feedback by connecting a time-varying voltage through a unity-gain "buffer" to an audio amplifier and speaker (see Figure 1).

Students in *CS4620* use two Departmental computers that are connected to a TCP/IP-based ethernet (*csnet*):

- **cs**, a dual-processor AlphaServer/2100A running Digital Unix, and

- **rt**, a Concurrent Computer Corporation SLS 6450 using the Real-Time Unix operating system.

Cs is used for compute-intensive processing and visualization whereas **rt** is primarily used for real-time data acquisition. Students access these machines from color and monochrome X11 terminals available in the Department, from across campus using Appalachian's fiber-based network, or through dial-up serial and PPP/SLIP connections.

Additional software "tools" have been added to the course to provide a more complete real-time software development environment. In addition to using the C programming language on both **cs** and **rt**, students also have access to visualization (**gnuplot**) as well as numeric (**octave**) and symbolic (**Maple**) computation systems. These packages are discussed in the next section.

In order to gradually introduce more complex topics in sound synthesis, labs are included to generate a single pure tone (**wave** and **pitch**), a sound with richer harmonic content (**timbre**), and finally a sequence of notes changing over time (**tune**). Each of these labs is described in Section 4.

2 Tools

Real-time data acquisition programs are usually written in assembly language or a higher-level language (HLL) such as FORTRAN, C, C++ or ADA. Using additional software tools in conjunction with a HLL real-time implementation has been found to be extremely effective in teaching real-time topics. The purpose of this section is to introduce this additional software used in *CS4620*. Space does not permit a detailed explanation of these packages. Instead, the interested reader is encouraged to consult the references for more information.

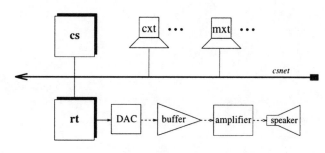

Figure 1: Sound Synthesis Hardware

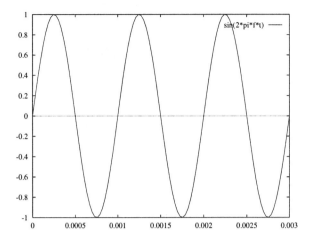

Figure 2: **gnuplot** graph of $\sin(2\pi 1000t)$

2.1 Gnuplot

Visualization has become an important part of modern computation. The ability to quickly create two- and three-dimensional plots of mathematical functions as well as textual and binary data is provided by the free **gnuplot** [22] program. Versions of **gnuplot** exist for Unix, Macintosh and Windows platforms.

Users can either enter commands interactively or place instructions in command files. Ease of use is possibly the most outstanding feature of this tool. For example, to create a graph of the cosine function on a default interval, only the following single interactive command is needed:

```
gnuplot> plot cos(x)
```

To create a Postscript file, `plot.ps`, containing the graph of both a sine and cosine between -2π and $+2\pi$, the following is entered:

```
gnuplot> set terminal postscript
gnuplot> set output "plot.ps"
gnuplot> plot [-2*pi:2*pi]
               sin(x), cos(x)
```

Gnuplot is the first "tool" introduced to the students of *Real-Time Systems*. Early homework assignments use the program to graph trigonometric series. Later in the course, they produce visualizations of waveforms to ensure that the coding of these waveforms corresponds to requirements. Here is an example of the commands used to plot the first few periods of a 1 kHz sine wave (see Figure 2):

```
gnuplot> f = 1000
gnuplot> plot [t=0:.003]
               sin(2*pi*f*t)
```

Gnuplot lacks the ability to save the data points generated. This capability is needed by students when creating the discrete samples used to generate analog signals via the DAC. Though C programs could be written (and have in past years) to generate such data, another tool, **octave**, is now used for this purpose.

2.2 Octave

Octave [7] is a free, high-level language for numeric processing similar to MATLAB [11, 10]. Like MATLAB, the basic data type in **octave** is a matrix. Many built-in functions are provided to manipulate one- and two-dimensional arrays. In addition, features are included for common control structures, reading and writing arrays (text and binary), defining user functions, and plotting. In fact, **octave** internally invokes **gnuplot** as a sub-process for all its graphics functions.

Commands in **octave** are terminated with or without a semi-colon. The latter indicates a request to display the results of the command whereas the former indicates that no output is desired (useful when defining large arrays). For example, consider the following commands that create a 3x3 identity matrix, A:

```
octave> n = 3;
octave> A = eye(n)
A  = 1 0 0
     0 1 0
     0 0 1
```

Note that the value of n was not displayed since the line initializing n is terminated with a semi-colon. However, since the command creating the matrix A ends with no semi-colon, the values of all of its elements are shown.

Without guidance, students tend to write **octave** code in a manner similar to that of C and other HLLs (e.g., explicit use of subscripts). This approach fails to take advantage of one of the main features of **octave** and other numeric processing systems: very efficient calculations on vectors and arrays. Most of the more advanced array calculations are performed in **octave** by well-known libraries including LINPACK/LAPACK [8, 5], FFTPACK [19], and ODE-PACK [12].

As a second example of **octave** code, consider the following commands to plot the earlier graph consisting of the first few periods of a 1 kHz sine wave:

```
octave> f = 1000;
octave> t =
       linspace(0.000,0.003,256);
octave> y = sin(2*Pi*f*t);
octave> plot(t,y);
```

This example shows the power of **octave**'s matrix data types. What would normally be programmed as a loop in a HLL (including a declaration of the loop variable) is here done implicitly. In addition, unlike **gnuplot**, the above commands allow the retention of the generated values. The efficiency of implicit matrix loops is even greater when performing more compute-intensive matrix operations such as products, inverses, convolutions and the fast Fourier transform [17].

2.3 Maple

The final "tool" used by students of *Real-Time Systems* is **Maple** [14, 2, 1], a computer algebra system (CAS). Though **Maple** is capable of performing numeric calculations and producing high-quality plots, its primary strength lies in its ability to manipulate mathematical symbols.

For example, consider factoring the third-order polynomial,

$$p(x) = x^3 + 11x^2 + 31x + 21.$$

This is accomplished using the following **Maple** statements:

```
> p := x -> x^3 + 11*x^2
                + 31*x + 21:
> factor(p(x));
            (x + 3)(x + 7)(x + 1)
```

Note that **Maple**, like **octave**, allows optional display of results. Terminating a statement with a colon suppresses output.

Computer science majors at Appalachian State University are required to take two semesters of calculus along with linear algebra and statistics. Because *CS4620* is a senior/graduate course and taken late in their academic career, many of the students have not used any advanced mathematics since taking calculus courses in their first year.

For this reason, *Real-Time Systems* reviews some basic elements of trigonometry and calculus including trigonometric identities, the chain rule for differentiation, and integration-by-parts before presenting material on Fourier series and analysis. Our students understand that CASs are ineffectual unless the user knows and understands mathematics. Given this knowledge and understanding, **Maple** permits the rote work of mathematical symbolic manipulation (e.g., factoring, simplification, and expansion) to be performed by a computer.

Maple is used in the Department's real-time course while discussing the derivation of the coefficients of the Fourier expansion of mathematical functions on the interval $[-\pi, +\pi]$. After the Fourier series,

$$\frac{a_0}{2} + \sum_{n=1}^{\infty} (a_n \cos nt + b_n \sin nt) \qquad (1)$$

and its coefficients,

$$a_0 = \frac{1}{\pi} \int_{-\pi}^{\pi} f(t)\, dt$$

$$a_n = \frac{1}{\pi} \int_{-\pi}^{\pi} f(t) \cos nt\, dt, \qquad n = 1, 2, \ldots \qquad (2)$$

$$b_n = \frac{1}{\pi} \int_{-\pi}^{\pi} f(t) \sin nt\, dt, \qquad n = 1, 2, \ldots$$

are presented, an application is discussed. This in-class example derives the Fourier expansion of,

$$f(t) = t, \qquad t \in [-\pi, +\pi]. \qquad (3)$$

Due to the simplicity of $f(t)$, the mathematics is straightforward though somewhat verbose.

A homework assignment is then given to calculate the Fourier coefficients of another function,

$$g(t) = t^2, \qquad t \in [-\pi, +\pi].$$

Unlike equation (3), this function's first derivative (useful during integration-by-parts) does not reduce to a constant. Thus, the mathematical manipulation is more complicated. Many students use **Maple** for this assignment.

For example, here is a portion of a **Maple** (release 2) worksheet that calculates the coefficient a_n (2) associated with the nth cosine term of the Fourier series expansion (1) of $g(t)$:

```
> g := t -> t^2:
> a := n ->
        (1/Pi)*int(g(t)*cos(n*t),
        t=-Pi..Pi);
```

$$a := n \to \frac{1}{\pi} \int_{-\pi}^{\pi} t^2 \cos(nt)\, dt$$

```
> simplify(a(n));
```

$$2\frac{-2\sin(n\pi) + n^2 \sin(n\pi)\pi^2 + 2n\cos(n\pi)\pi}{\pi n^3}$$

```
> subs(sin(n*Pi)=0,");
```

$$4\frac{\cos(n\pi)}{n^2}$$

```
> subs(cos(n*Pi)=(-1)^n,");
```

$$4\frac{(-1)^n}{n^2}$$

Besides simplifying the derivation of coefficients, many students also use **Maple**'s *plot* function to show, in fact, that the derived Fourier series is correct.

3 Data acquisition software

Concurrent's Real-Time Unix (RTU) operating system includes a robust software environment for real-time processing. Facilities exist for inter-process communication, process synchronization, and asynchronous system traps (ASTs). Various transfer methods are available to support real-time, simultaneous, multi-channel data acquisition using **rt**'s high-speed (up to 4 MHz sampling rate) analog-to-digital and digital-to-analog converters. An extensive library (*mr*) is provided to facilitate implementation of diverse real-time applications.

3.1 Transfer methods

All of the sound synthesis labs require the transfer of two's complement discrete values to the DAC. As students become familiar with the RTU environment and the concepts of real-time computation, the more advanced data transfer methods are employed.

3.1.1 Memory

The simplest and least flexible of the transfer methods provided is the *memory transfer* method. This consists of placing the required discrete samples within an integer-aligned vector of C **short**s. Once the data is in the vector, a library routine is called to perform the transfer using the system's direct memory access (DMA) hardware.

Though easy to use, this methods suffers from two shortcomings. First, the time duration of the discrete data is limited by available primary memory (M_p) which is consumed quickly using the digital audio standard sampling rate of 44.1 kHz. For example, three minute single channel CD-quality sound requires a data vector of 15,876,000 bytes (180 seconds × 44100 Hertz × 2 bytes per sample). The second problem is that an executing application does not have access to the vector once a transfer has been initiated. This precludes any real-time processing of the vector's contents (e.g., generating a continuous signal whose frequency varies over time). The additional transfer methods provide techniques to overcome both of these limitations.

3.1.2 File

Since **rt** has only 16MB of M_p, there is insufficient room for RTU and an application with demanding memory requirements. Though the real-time machine supports paging and swapping through its virtual memory system, these mechanisms must be suspended on a process-by-process basis during real-time data acquisition to guarantee uninterrupted data transfer.

To overcome limited M_p, the *mr* library supports a second method of data transfer utilizing contiguously-allocated binary disk files. With only slight changes to an application, a program can be modified to perform DMA transfers directly from a file to a DAC. An additional feature supporting the *file transfer* method is RTU's "disk-locked" processes. This ensures that a real-time process has exclusive use of the controller interface connected to the disk containing raw data samples.

3.1.3 Buffered

The most dynamic of all transfer methods is the *buffered transfer*. This approach, like the memory transfer method above, uses a single large vector in primary memory. Thus it also shares that method's limitation of a restricted discrete sample vector length. The advantage of this method, however, is that the single data vector is divided into many (at least five) sub-vectors or buffers which are processed in first-in/first-out order.

Using a three-tiered (user process, device driver, and hardware device) scheme of buffer lists and queues allows an application to process non-busy ("done") buffers in real-time. As each buffer is released, its contents may be manipulated as long as the required processing time does not exceed the average buffer transfer time. For example, data being digitized from a microphone might be transformed by a digital filter to remove unwanted background noise. RTU communicates the fact a new buffer is available by issuing an AST to the user process.

3.2 Library

The structure of most RTU data acquisition programs is quite similar and independent of the data transfer method used. Programs consist of four major structural divisions: *preparation*, *setup*, *execution*, and *termination* [4]. RTU's *mr* library provides C functions (see Tables 1 and 2) and FORTRAN subroutines that permit easy implementation of these program divisions.

3.2.1 Preparation

This short section of a data acquisition program allocates space for a data vector ensuring that it is **int**-aligned for the most efficient transfer of data to the conversion device. This is accomplished by using a C **union**:

```
union {
  short sample[1024];
  int   dummy;
} buf;
```

Code within this section also ensures that required C header files are included, declares and initializes other application

mropen	Open device
mrclk1	Set clock frequency
mrwire	Associate clock with device
mrlock	Lock process in main memory

Table 1: *Setup* Real-Time Functions

mrdaxout	Transfer samples from memory
mrxoutf	Transfer samples from file
mrxoutq	Transfer samples using queues
mrevwt	Suspend until event variable $\neq 0$

Table 2: *Execution* Real-Time Functions

variables, and initializes any needed signal or AST handlers.

3.2.2 Setup

The next step is to identify and initialize all needed real-time devices with the *mropen* function. *Mropen* returns a non-negative value to uniquely identify each device in a manner similar to Unix file routines. These devices typically include at least one real-time clock and the DAC.

Additional setup includes specifying the frequency of all clocks (e.g., conversion frequency) with a call to the *mrclk1* (or other clock) function and indicating how the clocks are internally connected to data conversion devices through use of the *mrwire* function. Finally, a call to *mrlock* requests RTU to "lock" the real-time process in memory. In other words, once this function has returned, all of the issuing process' memory pages are forced to remain resident in M_p. As described earlier, allowing swapping and/or paging during high-speed data acquisition must be avoided.

3.2.3 Execution

At this point, a program is ready to begin transferring data. The function invoked depends on the transfer method. *Mrdaxout* begins transfer of data from a vector of discrete samples to one or more DAC channels. Applications needing a larger vector of samples use the *mrxoutf* function to initiate the movement of samples from a contiguous disk file to the DAC. Finally, those programs which need to manipulate the samples before transfer use the *mrxoutq* library function.

Each of these three "data transfer" functions has a similar calling sequence. In particular, they first specify parameters indicating the conversion device and either one or two clocks. Multiple clocks are used for "burst" mode wherein a "frame" of samples is periodically transfered. The first clock specifies the data conversion frequency and the second the "frame frequency" (i.e., how often to convert the next "frame" of data).

Following the device specifiers are parameters indicating how multiple conversion channels are used. This information includes the starting channel number, the number of channels to convert, and a "channel increment". This last parameter allows, for example, performing transfers to/from only odd-number channels. The final arguments to

the functions specify the number of conversions to perform and the address of the discrete data vector.

Once one of the above three functions has initiated a data transfer, the *mrevwt* function is invoked. Since transfers proceed asynchronously, a process must have a mechanism to indicate when each transfer has completed. RTU communicates this through the use of an "event variable". *Mrevwt* suspends execution of a program until an event variable associated with a transfer becomes non-zero. Once this occurs, a program typically re-invokes the transfer function thus permitting continuous data conversion.

3.2.4 Termination

Once all data acquisition activities have completed, a program simply closes all real-time devices using the *mrclose* function. In addition, any other "cleanup" is performed including flushing file buffers as well as closing files.

4 Labs

Real-Time Systems uses sound as a familiar, convenient, and interesting physical phenomenon from which to learn the concepts and methods of real-time data acquisition. The first few weeks are spent learning about digital input/output and finite state machines [13]. Then, students turn to the analog output portion of the course. After a brief introduction to digital-to-analog conversion and its hardware, the first analog lab is assigned.

4.1 Wave

Students must write a program, **wave** (see Figure 3), which uses "command line arguments" to specify a continuous waveform. These arguments specify the following characteristics needed to generate a periodic waveform:

- Type (sinusoid, triangle or "mystery"),

- Frequency (Hertz),

- Duration (seconds), and

- D/A conversion frequency (Hertz).

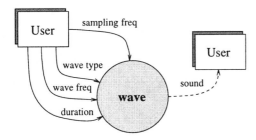

Figure 3: **wave** Context

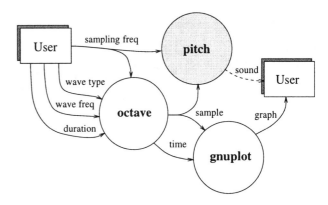

Figure 4: **pitch** Context

The output of **wave** is an analog voltage (shown as a dashed line in Figure 3) produced by a call to the *mrdaxout* function. The frequency and amplitude of the required waveform is verified with an oscilloscope. Later labs connect the DAC's output to an amplifier and speaker. The purpose of this lab is to acquaint students with basic digital-to-analog conversion as well as giving them experience in coding discrete sample generation in a familiar language (C).

The following ANSI C code fragment generates x(n), the required vector of two's-complement samples for the *sinusoidal* wave type:

```
T = 1.0/sampling_freq;
num_of_samples = duration
                 *sampling_freq;
omega = 2*M_PI*wave_freq;
for(n=0; n<num_of_samples; n++)
  x[n] = (short)MAXSAMPVAL
                 *sin(omega*n*T);
```

Students are encouraged to reflect on the difference between discrete (nT) and continuous (t) time domains.

4.2 Pitch

Following completion of the **wave** project, students are introduced to **octave**. An entire lab period is spent learning the basic features of **octave** including simple matrix manipulation and graphing. After the class is comfortable using this package, the next lab (**pitch**) is assigned (see Figure 4).

This program is similar to **wave**. However **octave** is now used to generate the discrete samples (instead of C) and **gnuplot** is used to produce various visualizations. Once the data vector is verified in "time vs. amplitude" graphs, it is output to a binary file using **octave**'s *fwrite* function. This data file is then transfered to **rt** and input by a C program. Using the *mrxoutq* data transfer function, **pitch** produces a continuously running output voltage that is then amplified and played through a speaker or headphones.

Students soon grow weary of the constant pitch of the sound. Fortunately, lecture material shifts to Fourier series and the production of more complex waveforms using multiple harmonics of a fundamental frequency. Thus, strong

motivation and background material are provided for studying and implementing techniques of the next lab.

4.3 Timbre

Since most Appalachian State University computer science majors have no background in Fourier analysis, they are gently introduced to the topic by an applied approach in the **timbre** lab (see Figure 5). Students are provided with photocopies of "amplitude spectrum" graphs copied from various musical texts. They must pick one from among three spectra of musical instruments (cello, trumpet and clarinet) [6] and one of five spectra of a violin string "plucked" at various locations [16]. In addition, they are asked to randomly generate (using coins) a third spectrum.

Once each student has chosen two spectrum graphs and created a random spectrum, the amplitudes of all significant harmonics on the graphs are measured. These spectra are input by an **octave** program which first converts the measurements from decibels to linear, normalized amplitude. (Note that the phase component of each harmonic is ignored.)

Each converted amplitude in a spectrum is used as the coefficient of a term in a Fourier series (with a fundamental frequency of 880 Hz) which when evaluated over a time interval and summed, generates a discrete time signal. As in the last lab, the data is then written into a binary file, transfered to **rt**, converted by the DAC at 44.1 kHz, and eventually heard on the speaker.

Most students are impressed with the noticeable differences in timbre between each instrument and violin "plucking" positions. Not surprisingly, they are also convinced that a random collection of harmonics does not necessarily produce a sound that is pleasing to the ear.

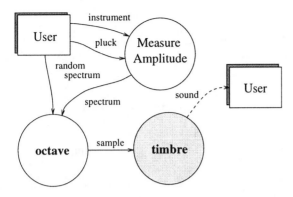

Figure 5: **timbre** Context

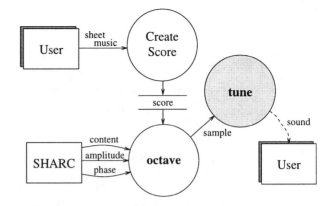

Figure 6: **tune** Context

4.4 Tune

Even though the sounds produced by **timbre** are more interesting than a tone of constant pitch, students soon find even the richer content boring. The next step is to create a system, **tune**, which permits variations of timbre over time (see Figure 6).

The project begins by giving each student sheet music of a short melody. After a talk on musical notation, students are asked to convert the sheet music into a "score file". This ASCII file consists of an initial integer specifying the melody's tempo (or meter) as the number of milliseconds in a quarter note. Each subsequent line specifies either a "note" or a "rest" along with a duration (whole, half, quarter, eight). For example, here is a sample "score" which plays the first three notes of a C major scale followed by a quarter rest:

```
128
c4      q
d4      q
e4      q
-       q
```

Students interested in this approach to music creation are encouraged to investigate the much more robust **Csound** [21] and **Cmusic** [15] electronic music systems.

Significant additional work remains in order to convert these "scores" into actual sound. Rather than using approximate spectral measurements as done in the previous lab, students are told to utilize the huge database of 39 orchestral instruments known as the *Sandell Harmonic Archive* (SHARC) [18]. Once each student has chosen an instrument from the many available, "symbolic links" are created in a sub-directory of the **tune** project on **cs** for the corresponding files.

The SHARC data is organized into separate directories — one for each of the 39 instruments (e.g., french horn, bass trombone, bassoon, tuba, oboe, piccolo, ...) in the archive. Each instrument directory contains a single "contents" file and multiple "note" files. The first file contains an index of notes available for the given instruments (e.g., a#3, b3, c3, ...). Lines within the "contents" file consist of a note name (from the Acoustical Society of America standard), its frequency in Hertz [9], and the number of harmonics contained within each of the respective "note" files. These later files contain multiple lines each consisting of the value of amplitude and phase for each harmonic.

Once the students understand the structure and content of SHARC, they write an **octave** program that reads each line of the "score" file. If the next sound is a rest, their program generates a sequence of zero-valued time data.

On the other hand, if the next line specifies a note, they use the SHARC harmonic data for that note to generate an appropriate wave shape by substituting the amplitude and phase from each harmonic into a Fourier series whose fundamental frequency is specified in the "contents" file. Once an entire tune has been synthesized, discrete samples are written into a binary file and eventually "played" on the real-time hardware.

5 Conclusion

Teaching real-time data acquisition is enhanced through the use of supplementary software "tools" in addition to traditional programming environments. This paper introduced examples of such software packages (**gnuplot**, **octave**, and **Maple**) and presented details of a real-time data acquisition library. It also described a series of four labs demonstrating the use of these "tools" to produce successively higher-quality sound: a pure tone, a "richer" tone consisting of a few harmonics, and a high-fidelity melody synthesized from amplitude and phase values obtained from an orchestral harmonic database.

References

[1] Nancy R. Blachman and Michael J. Mossinghoff. *Maple V Quick Reference*. Brooks/Cole, 1994.

[2] Bruce W. Char et al. *First Leaves: A Tutorial Introduction to Maple V*. Springer-Verlag, New York, 1992.

[3] Ben E. Cline. *An Introduction to Automated Data Acquisition*. Petrocelli Books, New York, 1983.

[4] Concurrent Computer Corporation. *Data Acquisition Application Programming Manual*. Tinton Falls, NJ, 1991.

[5] J. J. Dongarra et al. *LINPACK User's Guide*. S.I.A.M., Philadelphia, PA, 1979.

[6] Alan Douglas. *Electronic Music Production*. Tab Books, Blue Ridge Summit, PA, 1974.

[7] John W. Eaton. *Octave – a high-level language for numerical computations*. http://www.che.wisc.edu/octave/, Madison, WI, 1997.

[8] G. H. Golub and C. F. Van Loan. *Matrix Computations*. Johns Hopkins University Press, Baltimore, MD, 2nd edition, 1993.

[9] David E. Gray, W. Craig McKnight, and Stephen R. Wood. Audible Frequency Detection and Classification. In *Mississippi State DSP Conference Proceedings*, Mississippi State, MI, Fall 1996.

[10] Duane Hanselman and Bruce Littlefield. *Mastering MATLAB*. Prentice-Hall, Upper Saddle River, NJ, 1996.

[11] Duane Hanselman and Bruce Littlefield. *The Student Edition of MATLAB Version 5: User's Guide*. Prentice-Hall, Upper Saddle River, NJ, 1997.

[12] A. C. Hindmarsh. ODEPACK, A Systematized Collection of ODE Solvers. In *Scientific Computing*. North-Holland, Amsterdam, 1983.

[13] Kenneth H. Jacker. Real-Time Instructional Technology: Experiences with Multi-User Real-Time Systems. In *Real-Time Systems Education*. IEEE Computer Society Press, Los Alamitos, CA, 1996.

[14] M. B. Monagan et al. *Maple V Programming Guide*. Springer-Verlag, New York, 1997.

[15] F. Richard Moore. *Elements of Computer Music*. Prentice-Hall, Englewood Cliffs, NJ, 1990.

[16] Michael J. Moravcsik. *Musical Sound*. Paragon House, New York, 1987.

[17] Robert W. Ramirez. *The FFT: Fundamentals and Concepts*. Prentice-Hall, Englewood Cliffs, NJ, 1985.

[18] Gregory J. Sandell. *SHARC Timbre Database*. http://sparky.parmly.luc.edu/sandell/sharc/ SHARC.homepage.html, Chicago, IL, 1997.

[19] P. N. Swarztrauber. Vectorizing the FFTs. In *Parallel Computations*. Academic Press, San Diego, CA, 1982.

[20] Arnold H Vandoren. *Data Acquisition Systems*. Reston, Reston, VA, 1992.

[21] Barry Vercoe. *Csound: A Manual for the Audio Processing System and Supporting Programs with Tutorials*. M. I. T., Cambridge, MA, 1992.

[22] Thomas Williams and Colin Kelley. *gnuplot*. http://www.cs.dartmouth.edu/gnuplot/gnuplot.html, Hanover, NH, 1997.

A Student Project in the Field of Satellite Tracking

M. Barbeau

Département de mathématiques et d'informatique
Université de Sherbrooke
Sherbrooke, Québec, CANADA J1K 2R1
www.dmi.usherb.ca/~barbeau

Abstract

This paper presents a project given to the students of a real-time system course. The project consists of developing a software for tracking in real-time non geostationary satellites. Students have to analyze, design, program, and test their solution. The project is not solely a simulation. There is a satellite tracking lab where students can really experiment and validate their solution. This paper presents the problem given to the students, the hardware platform, and some elements of a typical solution.

1. Introduction

This paper presents a project given to the students of a course entitled Real-Time Systems that has been offered for the first time at the fall 1996 semester at University of Sherbrooke. The course is part of the curriculum of a Master of Software Engineering. This course aims to render the students apt to the realization of real-time systems by using methods of development and tools specific to this type of systems. More specific objectives are to make the students capable of understanding characteristics of real-time systems and to apply a method for real-time system development to a concrete problem. The course lasts one semester and consists of lectures, both given by the professor and students, and a major project. This paper is about the project given to the students.

There are several areas where systems have real-time characteristics. For this course, we chose the exciting one of satellite telecommunications. In their project, students develop a case study in the area of tracking in real-time non geostationary satellites. They perform a full software development project: analysis, design, implementation, and test. Each student develops its own solution.

The suggested development framework is the object-oriented development methodology of Booch [2]. The reason we use Booch is because it explains very well how to tackle the different development phases (in particular analysis, design, and implementation). The expected results of each phase are also very well described. One the flaws of the Booch approach, however, is the non executability of the analysis and design models. Verification through simulation, before implementation, is therefore not possible. Hence, although the Booch methodology is employed, the modeling language used for the project is ROOM [5]. The modeling language of ROOM has been devised specifically for real-time systems. It is very well documented and supported by a tool called ObjecTime. ObjecTime allows editing of models as well as verification through simulation. Automatic code generation is also possible, although not exploited in the course. Rather, students translate their ROOM model into C and C++ and program the implementation for the QNX real-time operating system [4]. The rest of the paper is organized as follow. Section 2 describes the problem given to the students. The hardware platform for the implementation of their solution is described in Section 3. Some elements of a typical solution are given in Section 4. We conclude with Section 5.

2. The Problem

The problem given to the students is in the area of telecommunications satellite tracking. This topic is very actual, relevant, and motivating. Telecommunications satellites can be classified into two categories (see Figure 1) according to whether or not they place the spacecraft in a geostationary orbit. A geostationary orbit is characterized by the fact that the equatorial and orbital planes coincide. Moreover, the satellite describes a circle around the earth at an altitude of approximately 35 680 km. These conditions are such that the satellite performs a complete cycle in every day, as well as the earth. Thus from the point of view of an observer on the ground, at a given location, the satellite is always at the same position in the sky. Tracking of geostationary satellites is trivial.

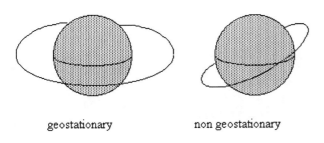

Figure 1: Types of orbits

The satellites in which we are interested in the student project are rather of the non geostationary type. The orbital and equatorial planes do not coincide and the first is inclined with respect to the second. The National Oceanographic and Atmospheric Administration (NOAA) [www.noaa.gov] maintains series of weather satellites on non geostationary orbits. Their altitude is relatively low (e.g.,: 850 km) and weather images can be received with relatively simple equipment [6]. In addition, AMSAT [www.amsat.org] (and other related voluntary organizations) maintains a series of non geostationary satellites, called Orbiting Satellite Carrying

Amateur Radio (OSCAR), which can be used as relays in different modes of transmission (analog or digital) [3]. Both reception and transmission are possible through them (an amateur radio license is required for transmission [www.rac.ca, www.arrl.org]).

Figure 2 illustrates the coverage of a typical non geostationary weather satellite. The area in which the satellite is visible from the earth is delimited by the ovoid figure. The latter is called the acquisition circle. Most of these satellites are at a relatively low altitude. It means that the acquisition circles of satellites of this type are of small dimension. The small cross indicates the place on the ground directly under the satellite. This point is called the subsatellite point (ssp). Because of the fact that the earth rotates on itself (and other phenomena), given a latitude and direction in which the satellite moves (up or down), the longitude of the ssp is shifted to the west from one cycle to another. It allows the satellite to cover all the surface of the earth during a certain period of time (e.g., a day). In Figure 2, the curved line indicates the future trace of the ssp for a cycle beginning from the current ssp.

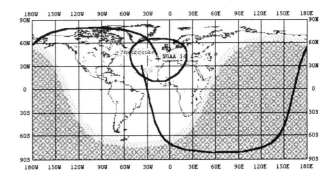

Figure 2: Orbit of a non geostationary satellite

To be able to communicate with a non geostationary satellite, it is necessary to determine at what time our position on the ground will be part of an acquisition circle. Directional antennas equipped with motors to adjust in real time their orientation may be required for communicating because the distance may be to great or the signal may be to weak. If directional antennas are necessary, we have to determine in real time in which direction they have to be oriented in terms of azimuth (an angle between zero and 360 degrees) and elevation (an angle between zero and 180 degrees). To make these calculations, a mathematical model of satellite orbits has to be implemented. A two-body mathematical model is well documented in Refs. [3] and [1]. Besides, the mathematical model has to be fed with data, called orbital elements. The mathematical model predicts the position of a satellite at a given time from coordinates observed at a time of reference. In order for this prediction to be the most accurate as possible, orbital elements have to be the most recent as possible. One can obtain them thanks to the Internet on the Web site of AMSAT (www.amsat.org) or the FTP site of Air Force Institute of Technology (archive.afit.af.thousand/pub/space/tle.new).

The problem given to students is the development of software for tracking in real time non geostationary satellites. Coding techniques and frequencies of NOAA and OSCAR spacecrafts are of the public domain. They can be worked out with relatively modest radio equipment. They are therefore really great for experimenting satellite communications. Students are challenged to experiment and validate their satellite tracking software with NOAA and OSCAR satellites. Development of a real-time satellite tracking software makes a great course project because it requires quite deep analysis and design. The size of the program, in terms of lines of code, is relatively modest, and the problem has soft real-time as well as hard real-time facets. In addition, validation of the result is possible with a not costly to set up satellite tracking laboratory described in the next section.

Figure 3: Crossed yagi antennas

3. Hardware Platform

This section describes the hardware platform on which students develop and test their satellite tracking software. The communication equipment must be capable of communicating in the VHF (2 m) and UHF (70 cm) radio bands.

Directional antennas equipped with rotors, to adjust in real time their orientation, are required to communicate. An antenna for the 2 m band and another for the 70 cm band are necessary. The polarity of antennas of satellite is circular. Antennas on the ground can be of the type yagi (similar to broadcast television reception antennas) but those of type crossed yagi give best results. A crossed yagi possesses both a series of vertical elements and a series horizontal elements. Their gain is three decibels higher than a non crossed yagi because their polarity is equally circular. Antennas are mounted side by side on a horizontal cross boom. Figure 3 presents a system of antennas for the 2 m and 70 cm bands. It comprises crossed yagis for the 2 m and 70 cm bands. Their length is approximately 10 feet. Rotors are necessary to vary the azimuth and elevation of antennas in order to maintain their orientation in the direction of a satellite. The rotor system, pictured in Figure 3, is computer controlled. Antennas are mounted on a tripod installed on a flat roof of a building. Their height is not critical. It is, however, necessary that the path of transmission-reception be the most clear as possible.

Figure 4: Radio equipment

Preamplifiers make possible communication with antennas of shorter length. They have to be as close as possible to the antennas. Ideally on the mast in a case that is going to protect them from moisture. It is, however, necessary to keep in mind the fact that a preamplifier increases not only the amplitude of the signal but equally the noise. Its efficiency can be reduced considerably in urban areas. Thus, when these antennas are installed in an electromagneticly noisy environment, they have to be as long as possible (e.g., 15 feet). In contrast, for an installation in an environment where the level of the noise is moderate, antennas can be shorter (e.g., five to eight feet) and the signal can be strengthened by means preamplifiers. There exist radios specially devised for satellite communication in the 2 m and 70 cm bands. The most popular models are the ICOM IC-821, Kenwood TS-790, and Yaesu FT-736. These radios have several features that facilitate the task of the operator. Figure 4 presents the equipment of our satellite communication station. There is a Yaesu FT-736R radio covering the 2 m, 70 cm, and 23 cm bands. The station comprises also an AEA DSP-2232 digital signal processor to encode and decode the different signals employed by the satellites. Excluding the computer, we invested about 4 800$ US for the equipment (radio 2 000$ US, DSP 1 000$ US, antenna system 1 300$ US, and various harware pieces 500$ US).

4. Elements of a Solution

In this section, we discuss the highlights of a typical solution to the problem given to the students. A good design consists of a top level object with three sub objects (actors, in the language of ROOM). The top level object models the control flow of the application. The three sub objects are responsible of determining the ssp, calculating the azimuth and elevation of the satellite, and driving the antennas in the right direction. They are respectively called the groundTracker, azElProvider, and driver. The behavior of the top level actor is modeled by a ROOMchart (an extended state-transition diagram) triggered on a periodic basis by the expiration of a timer. It is initialized with fresh orbital elements of a satellite. When its behavior is triggered, it polls the groundTracker to obtain the current ssp and altitude of the satellite. Both values are passed to the azElProvider which returns the current azimuth and elevation of the satellite. Finally, the azimuth and elevation are transmitted to the driver that starts or stops the motors of the antennas in accordance to the difference between the current position and the target.

Separation of control, in the top level object, and functional aspects, in the sub objects, results in low coupling between the functional elements. Therefore, its makes them more reusable, in other contexts, and substitutable, by other functionally equivalent elements.

Design of the object groundTracker requires a deep understanding of a mathematical model of orbits. It is one of the difficult parts of the project. In the course, we spent two three hours lectures on that topic. There are several models but a simple two-body model (a model that takes into account solely the influence of the earth on one orbiting spacecraft) is popularized in Ref. [3]. More details can also be found in Ref. [1]. There are two levels of difficulties: designing a software that implements a mathematical model of circular orbits and designing one that implements a model of elliptical orbits. The former is relatively simpler than the latter. Both, however, require understating of tracking terms (e.g., inclination), spherical trigonometry, and astronomy concepts (e.g., sideral time). Implementation of an elliptical model is more challenging because the equations are more complex and computation of one of the intermediate values requires implementation of the Newton-Raphson method. In both cases, however, there is a challenge in the understanding of the mathematical model. The resulting program is quite small: a couple of pages. All students implemented a model limited to circular orbits.

Design of the azElProvider is more straightforward. This object determines where to point the antennas according the location of the ground station, ssp, and altitude of the satellite. Equations required for this part of the problem are documented in Ref. [3].

Design of the driver needs understanding of the hardware interface with antenna rotors. There are a couple of interface models available on the market. One of the difficulties we encountered in the project was to find a product with the companion documentation required for understanding programming of the card. The software has soft as well as hard real-time aspects. On the one hand, the top level object is triggered on periodic basis (e.g., every couple of seconds). Although, delays in providing the azimuth and elevation are not so critical since the antennas have a certain beam width. On the other hand, rotors of antennas strike a knock right after 360 degrees of azimuth or 180 degrees of elevation. When these positions are reached the motors do not stop by themselves and they may burn after a while. So care must be taken in the design of the driver to handle this situation. To diminish the risk of burning the motors, we developed an electronic box that simulates the rotors. For the initial test, we plug into the rotor interface card this box instead of the real rotors. This kind of hardware simulator is mandatory when such equipment is used in turn by several students. The software developed by students has to run on the QNX platform. QNX has several real-time features like fast context switching of processes and fast interprocess communication. There was, however, a lack of use by the students of features specific to QNX, like multiprocess implementation. Students developed their program on Sun work stations, with which they are already very familiar, then transfer it on QNX for the final testing.

5. Conclusion

This paper has presented a student project for a real-time system course. The problem consists of developing a software for tracking in real time non geostationary satellites. The development of a solution is a quite substantial piece of work and keeps students busy for a whole semester. At the beginning of the course, we assume that they already know C and C++ as well as a little about software engineering. In addition, they have to read about the Booch method, understand the ROOM model, learn the ObjecTime tool, acquire a deep understanding of a two-body satellite orbit model, understand the hardware, and finally they need to become familiar with QNX. We believe that acquisition of knowledge about so many things is typical of a real-time system development project. Not all students succeed to do the whole thing but most of them are highly motivated.

More information about ROOM and ObjecTime is available at the following URL www.objectime.on.ca. More information about QNX is available at the URL www.qnx.ca. AMSAT maintains a Web site containing orbital elements, technical descriptions of OSCAR satellites, and examples of tracking software (www.amsat.org). Information about states of OSCAR satellites, and other related spacecrafts, are available and updated on a weekly basis at the Web site www.cs.indiana.edu (look for file finger/pilot.njin.net/magliaco/w).

Acknowledgments

The author would like to thank Marc Normandeau and Gaston Sirois for their participation to the setting up of the satellite communication station of the University of Sherbrooke. Thanks also to Jean Bédard, who has taken the pictures, and Aubin Roy, that has developed the electronic simulator of the antenna rotors. Part of the ideas that are presented in this paper emerged from a research project, joint with Centre de recherche informatique de Montréal (CRIM), financially supported by the Natural Sciences and Engineering Research Council (NSERC) of Canada and Bombardier Inc.

References

[1] R. Bate, D. Mueller, and J. White, *Fundamentals of Astrodynamics*, Dover Publications Inc., New York, 1971.

[2] G. Booch, *Object-Oriented Analysis and Design with Applications*, Second Edition, Benjamin/Cummings, 1994.

[3] M. Davidoff, *The Satellite Experimenters Handbook*, The American Radio Relay League, 2nd Edition, 1994 (ISBN: 0- 87259-318-5).

[4] QNX Software Systems Ltd, *QNX 4 Operating System - System Architecture*, 1993.

[5] B. Selic, G. Gullekson, and P. T. Ward, *Real-time Object-oriented Modeling*, John Wiley & Sons, Inc. 1994 (ISBN: 0-471-59917-4).

[6] R. E. Taggart, *Weather Satellite Handbook*, The American Radio Relay League, 5th Edition, 1994 (ISBN: 0-87259-448-3).

Progress Toward an Inexpensive Real-Time Testbed
The Pinball Player Project*

Dayton Clark
Department of Computer
& Information Science
Brooklyn College/CUNY
Brooklyn, New York 11210
dayton@brooklyn.cuny.edu

Abstract

The Pinball Player Project is nearing completion of its first phase–construction of a working prototype. The immediate purpose of the project is to develop an inexpensive testbed for real-time programming–a device within reach financially and technically of any Computer Science or Computer Engineering department. This paper discusses the need for such a testbed and the rationale for the particular model (a pinball machine and a PC). We also report on the status of the project and our thoughts for dissemination and use of the testbed within the real-time educational community.

1 Introduction

The major programming or systems areas of Computer Science reached profound levels of maturity in the 1950's, 60's and 70's. That is, fundamental theoretical questions were posed and answered and significant tools were developed to exploit and complement the theory. Consider Table 1 which lists significant developments in several systems areas. The anomaly in Table 1 is computer networks, but by in large networks did not exist at all until the mid-to-late 60's.

The ability to control real-world processes by computer became a reality with the advent of the mini-computer at about the same time as the early networks, the mid-to-late 60's. Yet, even today, for developers of real-time systems there are very few tools available and very little consensus within the real-time community as to which tools. Even if one adjusts for the late start of real-time systems, the area seems overdue for galvanizing events like those in the Table 1.

The theory of scheduling real-time tasks has pro-

gressed nicely. There is wide-spread consensus on real-time scheduling algorithms. However, even here, the early date of the ground-breaking work (Liu and Layland in 1973 [liu73]) raises the question, where are the development tools?

The major reason for the slow maturation of the field is that real-time programming is difficult. The imposition of inviolable external time constraints increases the difficulty of "normal" programming in a qualitative manner. This cannot be over-emphasized. However, we feel that a significant contributor to the slow development of real-time programming is more mundane. Specifically, the problem is the lack of access to computer controlled real-time systems brought about by the high cost of such systems. This lack of access greatly reduces the number of programmers who are exposed to real-time systems in their education thereby reducing the general knowledge of and interest in the problems of real-time programming. Typical research into real-time systems and the attendant programming is in military, avionic, space or robotics where the devices are expensive and unavailable to many colleges and universities. They are expensive both in initial cost and in maintenance, requiring skilled personnel to keep them operational. An example of this is provided by the robotic hand developed by the University of Utah and MIT in the mid-1980's for use in research into robotic manipulation [3]. This exquisite device was an order of magnitude more expensive than the rather ordinary computer equipment needed for control experimentation and was consequently available at only a handful of laboratories across the country.

The goal of the Pinball Player project is to develop a complete package (control and development computer(s), the controlled device(s), sensors, actuators, interfaces, and basic software) that can be put

---

*This project was supported in part by a grant from the Office of Naval Research (N00014-96-1-1057), by PSC-CUNY Research Award Program (665006) and by Brooklyn College.

Area	Development	Date
Scientific Computing	FORTRAN	late 50's
	Standard numerical libraries	late 60's
Languages and Compiling	Backus-Naur Form	late 50's
	Algol	early 60's
	LL & LALR parsers	late 60's
Operating Systems	Synchronization	early 60's
	Virtual memory	late 60's
	Layering	late 60's
Database Systems	COBOL	early 60's
	Relational databases	early 70's
Artificial Intelligence	LISP (symbolic programming)	early 60's
	Frames	early 70's
Computer Networks	Arpanet	early 70's
	Internet protocols	early 80's
	OSI paradigm	early 80's

Table 1: Significant Developments in Various Systems Areas

together from commonly available items and without exceptional mechanical or electronic engineering for under US$10,000. The experiences gained from creating such a system will be shared with the academic and research communities at large so that many institutions can develop and expand on the initial system.

The next two sections present the rationale for the plant and computing platform chosen for the testbed. Section 4 describes the current state of the project. The following section describes our vision of how the Pinball Player could be used educationally. Finally, we draw some conclusions in Section 6.

2 Why Pinball?

Selection of an appropriate system to control is critical to the success of the testbed. The system must have a real-time component. In addition, the system must be inexpensive and safe and the control must be simple enough to be within the reach of students and complex enough to be challenging. There are also advantages in a system that can be controlled by humans as well as by a computer. If students are able to control the system themselves (i.e., as humans) the highest level problems and strategies can be intuitively grasped. Human controllers also provide a ready benchmark for the success of the computer controller. And finally, with a human controllable plant, investigation of control strategies involving human training of the computer controller is feasible.

Arcade type pinball machines fit all of the criteria. They are readily available and inexpensive (US$100 for some as-is machines to US$2,500 for new ones). They are safe and easily understood. The basic acts of tracking and hitting a ball are decomposable into

pieces appropriate for instruction. The problems of keeping a ball in play and strategies for high scores are replete with challenges. The ability to have the computer "watch" a human play, for training, is a simple extension of the basic computer/pinball machine interface.

The idea of "toy" plants for real-time laboratories is not new. Zhang etal. [zhang94] presented research based on model train system and the author is aware of at least one use of model trains to teach real-time programming. Surely sentimental favorites, model trains have significant drawbacks for use as general educational tools. Although the basic operation and setup is simple–millions of children have or have had them–the creation of a system that presents interesting scheduling problems is non-trivial. Furthermore, maintenance of a model train system while not requiring advanced skills does require devotion and care. Contrast this with pinball machines which are designed to work with minimal setup yet to operate for long periods in unfriendly environments with maintenance limited to the occasional dusting and emptying of coin boxes. Finally, once one has successfully scheduled a particular model train system, the opportunity for further investigation is limited (e.g., changing train lengths or optimizing train schedules). With a pinball machine, every play is different and one can always strive to lengthen the time balls are kept in play. Furthermore, enhancements such as using multiple balls or obtaining a higher score (as opposed to simply keeping the ball in play) are rich with problems beyond the basic pinball play.

Another source of toy testbeds is the many the

73

small mobile robots that are available commercially or can be constructed (see *Mobile Robots: Inspiration to Implementation* [jones93]). The emphasis in these systems is on the electro-mechanical design more than the computer control and the mechanical design is often meant to eliminate or side-step the need for time-critical control. The control of multiple cooperating or competing mobile robots would present many real-time control problems but for general ease of use and setup we have chosen the pinball machine.

3 What Platform?

The choice of which computer to use for control of the pinball machine is clear. The IBM PC and its clones are ubiquitous. Every school has some and probably many of them on hand. New PC's now cost under US$2,000 and old ones are often discarded long before they are unusable. Students and faculty are familiar with the normal operation of PC's. Adapters for control and sensing devices are plentiful and inexpensive. The architecture of the PC is open, which will facilitate the development of special purpose hardware. Note that our goal of developing a testbed that can be easily setup and maintained proscribes the extensive use of special purpose hardware. But, once a testbed system is installed we expect and encourage students and faculty to experiment with hardware modifications to the testbed. We know of no other computer that would serve as well as the testbed's computer.

Selection of appropriate software platform is not as straight forward as the hardware and is in fact very much an open question. We are currently using FreeBSD[1] a freely distributed version of Unix with its roots in BSD variant of Unix from the University of California at Berkeley. We are attracted to it because it is distributed in source form, it is familiar to us, and is inexpensive. FreeBSD has some support for real-time processes and supports a POSIX compliant threads library[2].

There are many operating systems for the PC architecture. We have considered the better known and a brief summary of our thoughts on them follows. The PC's native operating systems from Microsoft (DOS and the various Windows) and IBM (OS/2) are obvious choices. However, we feel it is important that the testbed's operating system be as open as possible. We feel it is important avoid hindering experimentation with hidden and/or immutable characteristics of a non-real-time operating system. So, despite their widespread familiarity we feel these operating systems are inappropriate. For similar reasons we are not using commercial versions of Unix (Solaris and SCO's

Figure 1: The pinball machine

Unix). Commercial real-time operating systems such as VxWorks by Windriver Systems are also possibilities, but we have opted not to use one of these because of their proprietary nature, lack of familiarity, and cost. There are other free Unix systems, most noticeably Linux, our choice in this cases is mostly a matter of our own familiarity.

It is important to recognize that our use of FreeBSD is not an endorsement of FreeBSD as a real-time operating system. Rather, with the soup of constraints and options available to us, we have found FreeBSD to be the most useful platform for developing the testbed. In fact, our difficulty in selecting an operating system goes to the root of the motivation for this project, namely that with respect to software there is little consensus as what tools should be used.

Our prototype version will be based on this platform but we fully expect that if the project is adopted by other institutions that other operating systems will be used. In particular we would hope that support arose for the standard PC operating systems, DOS and Windows, other free operating systems such as Linux, and hopefully for real-time operating systems.

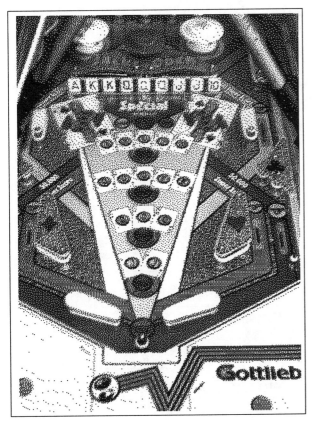

Figure 2: The pinball machine playing area

4 Current Status

This section describes the current status of the development of the prototype system. We present first the hardware, our pinball machine, control computer, the sensors and the actuators.

4.1 Hardware

The hardware in the prototype system consists of a pinball machine, a PC, a video input device, a digital and analog I/O board, and interface circuitry consisting of two relays connected to the pinball machine's flipper circuits (see Figure 3). The software consists of the operating system (modified slightly to support the sensors and actuators), our control software, and some initial control strategies.

4.1.1 The Pinball Machine

The plant for our prototype is a pinball machine called *Jacks to Open*. It was manufactured in the early 1980's by a company called Gottlieb. Figure 1 shows the pinball machine and Figure 2 shows the playing area.

The upper third of the playing surface consists of an obstacle course of bumpers and gates through which the ball must travel. The purpose of the area is to randomize the ball's behavior. The lower two-thirds of the playing area (roughly 45cm by 45cm) is mostly unobstructed with only a few bumpers and gates. At the bottom of this area are two flippers which guard the ball's main avenue of escape.

The only control available to the player is the flippers, each of which is controlled by a normally open switch located on the side of the machine. When a switch is closed the corresponding flipper is driven by a solenoid through an arc of about 90 deg to its "up" position. The flipper stays in this position until the switch is released. Control of the flipper is binary; there are no intermediate positions; it is either full on or full off.

4.1.2 Sensors

Pinball machines are designed to stimulate humans. There are a great many audible noises and flashing lights accompanying the play. Some of this activity provides information to the player such as the number of balls and games remaining, the current score, and "bonus" states in which certain actions further increase the player's score. It will be interesting in later stages of the project to track some of the auxiliary activities. At present we are exclusively interested in the ball's location so we can actuate the flippers at the appropriate times.

The pinball machine itself has several dozen sensors for keeping score and activating lights and sounds. There are sense switches in most of the gates. Many of the bumpers sense when the ball has struck them, Some of the obstacles sense when the ball strikes and then actively push the ball away. Our particular machine is monitored by a microprocessor (one would assume that this is true of all pinball machines manufactured in the last two decades). Tapping the sensor circuits is conceptually easy but it turns out that the information they provide is of little use when trying to hit the ball. Examination of Figure 2 shows that the top of the play area is densely populated with bumpers and gates and the lower portion (just above the flippers) is sparsely populated. Thus the machine's sensors provide little information about the ball's trajectory as it nears the flippers, precisely when we need it most.

So we are led to develop our own sensors. Our original plan was to avoid video input for two reasons. One reason was that video equipment tends to be more expensive, which was contrary to the goal of an inexpensive testbed. The second reason was that the immense problems of computer vision would likely overwhelm the control problems which are the purpose

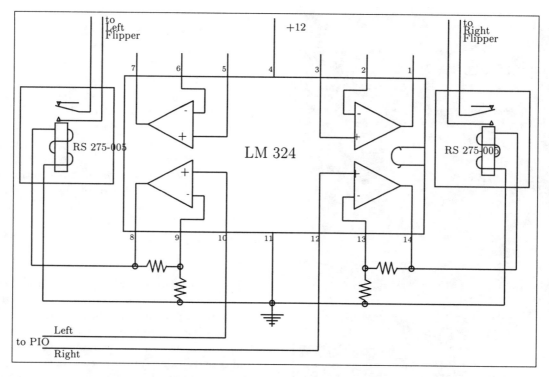

Figure 3: Circuitry connecting PIO to flippers.

of the testbed. Two experiences led us to reevaluate this choice. First, we experimented with various sensing schemes based on broken or reflected light beams with occasional but very sporadic good results. Second, as our frustration rose, small cameras for use in video conferencing over the Internet arrived on the market. These cameras, often shaped like billiard balls are connected directly to a computer's parallel port (no frame grabbing card), are able to deliver around $15\,frames/second$, and are very inexpensive (less than US$100 for a black and white camera).

We installed a *QuickCam* camera by Connectix and have had tremendous results. We can now track the ball in real-time using a very simple algorithm (see Figure 4). We detect motion by subtracting each image from its predecessor and thresholding. This yields a binary *difference* image which contains only the ball's locations in the two original images. A simple calculation using two of these difference images yields an image containing only the ball's current location. There are three drawbacks to this simple scheme. One is that the flippers also move so we need to distinguish them from the ball. At present, we simply ignore any activity in the immediate region of the flippers. Second, the pinball machine's own lights which flash at indeterminate times can fool our sensors. Our current solution is to turn off the machine's lights. Third,

shadows cast by someone walking near the machine may throw the sensor off. Our response is to stand clear of the machine while it is playing. We plan to implement a more sophisticated detection algorithm soon which we hope will overcome these disturbances.

4.1.3 Actuators

Each of the machine's flippers is driven by a 24 volt solenoid. When the input circuit is closed the solenoid pushes the flipper through an arc of approximately 90 deg. The flipper remains in this position until the circuit is opened. We have put a relay in the circuit, in parallel with the button used to activate the flipper. An output signal from a digital I/O board is amplified and becomes the input to the relay. The electronics are very simple and a program controls each flipper by toggling a bit on the I/O board.

A common question about the project is "How do you control the plunger which launches the ball into play"? At this time we don't. A device which would pull back the plunger and then let go to launch the ball would be interesting, but the problem is mostly a mechanical engineering problem and not of direct concern to us in this early phase of the project. An alternative would be to replace the plunger with a solenoid, which would launch the ball. We hesitate to take this

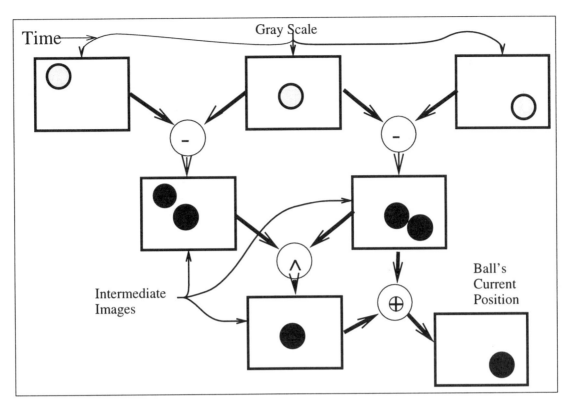

Figure 4: The Ball Tracking Algorithm

approach because one of our principles is to minimize modification of the machine itself. We adopt this principle because we want to ensure that the device we end up controlling is in fact a pinball machine, and it is not so extensively modified that is unrecognizable as such. However, to effectively measure and evaluate control systems and strategies we would like to have totally automatic play so that we can easily generate statistically significant data. This dilemma remains to be solved.

4.1.4 The Computer

Our current control computer is an IBM type PC with an Intel 486 processor running at $66Mhz$ with $16Mbytes$ of RAM. For input and output we have a *LabPC+* from National Instruments. The computer has an EISA bus and SCSI disks, but is otherwise a typical PC.

With this computer we are able to process 5 to 6 of the images each second. The ball on a top to bottom traversal of the viewing area takes .25 to .5 seconds. This yields 1 to 3 images of the ball as it traverses the viewing area. We are currently facing the challenge of developing control strategies to activate the flippers based on this sparse information.

When purchased, this machine was fairly powerful, but now is two generations old. This points out a difficulty confronting the long term prospects of this project and any attempt to develop real-time testbeds using simple physical systems. The cause of the difficulty is the exponential growth of processor speed over the last 30 years which shows no signs of slowing. The consequence is that a real-time system that has interesting and difficult time constraints today may be easily solved (at least for non-critical usage) a few years from now. As a consequence an educational institution must either maintain old computing equipment to keep the problem interesting or continually increase the complexity of the problems to be solved.

We envision some of both in the pinball player project. We have a multi-processor Pentium Pro system which we plan to use as a control computer also. Preliminary investigation indicates that one Pentium Pro processor will be able to process 15 images a second (the maximum output of the camera). Successfully controlling the flippers with this input is probably not trivial, but certainly will be easier than the 1 to 3 frames per second we get with the 486. We are purposely not using the more powerful system currently so that we can investigate the difference processor speed makes in the ability to control the pinball machine.

One solution to the phenomenon of ever increasing processor speed is to artificially hobble the processor with a high-priority *governor* process effectively reducing the processor's speed. Besides increasing the difficulty of the basic problem, a governor process would allow the processor's effective speed to be varied smoothly in order to pinpoint where particular control strategies or algorithms fail.

A variant of the governor process would be to add requirements to the basic problem such as keeping score of the game, producing a real-time graphical representation of the game in progress, or including the network in the control. A similar approach would be to increase the complexity of the overall strategy. Our current goal is to keep the ball in play as long is possible, so that the measure of success of a control program will be the seconds per ball or the number of hits per ball. Good human players play to maximize their scores, which is considerably more complicated than simply keeping the ball in play. If the control program is limited to visual input, playing for high score would be quite difficult indeed.

An inexpensive way to complicate the basic play is to add balls to the play. A second ball in the playing area would confound all but the most robust single ball controllers. The addition of subsequent balls would further complicate control, although at a diminishing rate. A more expensive way to a similar end would be to have the computer control multiple pinball machines simultaneously. Again one can measure either playing time or score.

A way to tighten time constraints would be to increase the angle of the playing area, causing the ball to fall faster through the playing area. This is probably of limited use though, since the ball's movements will become more predictable and the flippers less useful, as the angle of playing area increases.

Finally, one could emphasize the portability of a control system over its raw playing power. This would require several distinct pinball machines. The students would be charged with writing a controller using one or two machines for testing. Then the success of their controller would be measured on how quickly they can adapt their controller to a machine which they had not previously seen.

4.1.5 Control System and Strategies

Our control system is a multi-threaded program written in C. The user links the code for his or her strategy with this program. One thread obtains the input images and calculates the ball's position in the images.

Determining the corresponding position on the machine's playing surface is left to the strategy. Threads also control the flippers as commanded by the strategy.

We currently are working on three families of strategies for play; the Open-loop strategies, the Hot Spot strategies, and the FSM strategies. This list of families is not meant to exhaustively categorize possible strategies. It is merely a starting point for our work on control strategies.

The Open-loop strategies. The basic strategy in this family, discovered by the author's two year old, is to activate and deactivate the flippers rapidly and continuously. This strategy is surprisingly effective and results in a typical ball being hit one to three times before getting past the flippers.

Variables in this family include the rate at which the flippers are activated, how long the active state is held, and whether the two flippers are operated synchronously or asynchronously. One could also activate the flippers according to some pseudo-random sequence. Strategies from this family are useful as baseline strategies for comparison with other strategies.

The strategy of never activating the flippers is not without interest. It is true that on every play the ball would be hit back zero times, but the amount of elapsed time and the score obtained will vary. This is because the ball must pass through an obstacle course in the upper part of the playing surface. The amount of time taken to pass through the obstacle course and the score accumulated as the ball hits bumpers can vary considerably.

The Hot Spot Strategies. For this family the input image is partitioned into rectangular regions. Certain of the regions are designated as hot spots and if the ball is detected in one of these, activation of one or both flippers is scheduled. When the scheduled time arrives, the flipper or flippers is activated for a fixed interval.

This is the simplest class of closed loop strategies. Variations are obtained by modifying the granularity of the rectangular grid, the designate hot spots and the flipper scheduling intervals.

The FSM Strategies. This family is a generalization of the hot spot family which incorporates some history of the ball's trajectory. Again the input image is partitioned rectangles but now as the ball makes a transition from one rectangle to another a state change is triggered in a finite state machine maintained by the strategy. Entering a state of the FSM may optionally trigger the scheduling of a flipper, the cancelling of a scheduled flipper activation, or it may cause no action.

The number of variation within this family is immense. The grid size, the transitions, and the actions can all be varied. Increasing the size of the FSM incorporates more of the history of the ball's trajectory in each action decision.

5 Educational Use

As an educational tool the pinball player project has much promise. For introductory courses there are the basic problems of sensors, actuators, time-critical actions, and simple control strategies. For more advanced study there the problems can be enhanced with sophisticated control (e.g., achieving high score), multiple balls, multiple machines, graphical display, and remote play via the network. On the engineering side there is much that can be done to enrich the sensors. In particular, one can tap into the pinball machine's builtin sensing system. There is also much room for investigation into alternative software platforms.

An important aspect of the pinball project both educationally and as a testbed are the measurable quantities. Some of these quantities are:

- the number of times each ball is hit by the flippers;
- the amount of time that each ball remains in play;
- the score achieved for each ball or game of several balls;
- the number of balls that can be maintained in play;
- the number of machines that can be controlled;
- the time required to port a system to a new pinball machine; and
- the quality of play provided to a remote user.

This provides the instructor and/or student many avenues to explore within the framework of the basic pinball playing problem.

Contests. A measure of success of the pinball player project as a whole is how widely it is adopted as an educational tool. First of all, wide use of the pinball machine as a pedagogical tool will, we hope, foster a community of users who can share their experiences and accelerate the maturation of tools and strategies for using the system. One envisioned pedagogical strategy is to hold formal contests in which students from various institutions would match their systems (hardware and/or software) against each other under controlled circumstances. The areas for competition are sketched by the measurable quantities mentioned above.

6 Conclusions

In conclusion, we believe that an important factor in the slow maturation of real-time programming is the expense of purchase and maintenance of controllable systems (robots, cars, planes, etc.). The high cost prevents most colleges and universities from setting up a real-time laboratory. Consequently, most Computer Science students get minimal, if any, exposure to the problems of real-time systems. We propose that arcade type pinball machines provide an inexpensive, safe, accessible, interesting, and rich basis for real-time testbeds suitable for use as educational tool.

This paper describes our progress in creating a prototype pinball controller for educational use.

References

[1] *The FreeBSD Handbook*, http://www.freebsd.org, 1997

[2] IEEE, *POSIX 1003.1c/D12*, IEEE, New York, New York, 1995

[3] S.C. Jacobsen and J.E. Wood and D.F. Knutti and K.B. Biggers, "The Utah/MIT Dextrous Hand: Work in Progress", *International Journal of Robotics Research*, Vol. 3 No. 4, pp 21-50, 1984

[4] Richard Rashid and Robert Baron and Alessandro Forin and David Golub and Michael Jones and Daniel Julin and Douglas Orr and Richard Sanzi, "Mach: A Foundation for Open Systems" *Proceedings of the Second Workshop on Workstation Operating Systems(WWOS2)*, September 1989

[5] Lou Salkind, *SAGE: An Operating System for Real-Time Robotics Supervisory Control*, PhD Thesis, Courant Institute, New York University, 1989

[6] Andrew S. Tanenbaum, *Modern Operating Systems*, Prentice-Hall, Inc., Englewood Cliffs, New Jersey, 1992

[7] Joseph L. Jones and Anita M. Flynn, *Mobile Robots: Inspiration to Implementation*, A. K. Peters Wellesley, Massachusetts 1993

[8] L. Zhang and J. van Katwijk and K. Brink, "Applying Software Engineering Principles in Train Control Systems", *Second IEEE Workshop on Real-time Applications*, Washington, D.C., July 1994.

Creating a Virtual Lab for Real-Time Education on the Web

Cesar Munoz, Syed Rayhan, Tarik Iles, Janusz Zalewski
Department of Electrical and Computer Engineering
University of Central Florida. Orlando, FL 32816-2450

Abstract

Internet is geared toward the support of real time interactive applications where the users can establish video conferencing sessions, listen or watch radio/TV, and explore the real world through the remote acquisition and control of physical variables. Scientists and engineers are finding that remote experimentation can be conducted via Internet. This paper describes the UCF Virtual Lab Project, whose objective is to develop a Virtual Lab that allows professors and students to access and configure different laboratory instruments and control physical variables using a standard web browser.

1. Introduction

The Internet is growing in the range of applications that can be developed using its standard protocols: TCP/IP, HTTP, and HTML. Initially, Internet was used as a medium of delivering text information. The second phase was the establishment of some interaction using feedback forms and multimedia animation. Currently, Internet is geared toward the support of real-time interactive applications where the users can establish video conferencing sessions, listen or watch radio/TV, and explores the real world through the remote acquisition and control of physical variables.

Although Internet has bandwidth limitations and its protocols were not designed specifically to support these kind of real-time applications, an increasing number of universities and institutions are exploring the potential of the Internet in this area. Scientists and engineers are finding that important functions can be performed across the Internet. Several projects have been implemented to prove the viability of Internet to allow remote capture and control of real world variables like temperature or pressure, or devices like robots, video cameras, and so on. The following is a brief list of this kind of projects.

- A teleoperated robot. Department of Computer Science, University of Southern California [1]. An arm robot with a video camera can be manipulated remotely from a web browser.

- A remote weather station. National Instruments. Austin, Texas [2]. This project presents the real-time weather conditions in Austin Texas.

- A Simulated Nuclear Control Plant. Linkoping University. Linkoping, Sweden [3]. A Java applet simulates a failure sequence for a Nuclear power Plant.

- CMU Virtual Lab. Carnegie Mellon University [4]. This is an educational project to allow performing lab assignments using Internet.

- Second Best to Being There (SBBT). Oregon State University [5]. The goal of this project is to provide remote students with complete access to the undergraduate control engineering laboratory.

These projects are examples of a new paradigm that will become increasingly common in the work place: remote experimentation, which is the remote control and reconfiguration of instruments and control devices. An example of a workplace application is "an automated manufacturing line where an engineer can change parameters or troubleshoot remotely, saving the time and money of traveling to the plant. The growth of this paradigm will parallel the increasing use of telecommuting and teleconferencing"[6].

2. Project Description

The purpose of this project is to create a Virtual Lab environment where students and professors can conduct remote experiments through Internet. The project represents a first step to generate educational

80

and research interest in real-time remote experimentation in the Department of Engineering at the University of Central Florida.

Remote experimentation is a new paradigm in science, technology and education. Future engineers have to become familiar with an environment where some of the actual maintenance and troubleshooting will be done on-line and from remote location. Internet provides an inexpensive way to conduct remote experimentation, to access and to configure lab equipment from any location at any time. The specific goals are:

- Install and configure a data acquisition web server to allow monitoring and controlling physical variables (temperature, pressure, etc).

- Develop a set of Java programs (the Virtual Lab tool kit) to create the client user interface and to establish the communication between the client and the server. This tool kit will allow generating virtual lab assignments.

3. Virtual Lab Architecture

The UCF Virtual Lab is designed to monitor and control physical variables remotely.

A functional diagram representing the architecture of the system is shown in the in Figure 1.

Different kinds of sensors (temperature, pressure, and so on) are used to measure the current values of physical variables. These devices send the data to the server machine through a data acquisition board. The server machine reads and sends the recorded data to any remote Internet location with a web browser. The data can be visualized using a Java applet. The user can send control commands to the instruments or control devices from any web browser. The following is a brief description of the different components of the system.

The Data Acquisition Card (DAQ) provides the instrument's interface to the physical world. The DAQ contains digital and analog inputs/outputs that allow monitoring and controlling physical variables. The accuracy of the measurements depends on the resolution of the acquisition card.

The server machine hosts the HTTP and the data acquisition software. The data acquisition software contains the device drivers necessary to communicate with external sensors and instruments. The HTTP software is responsible for sending the result of the acquisition to the clients.

The client module runs on any remote computer with a web browser. The client software is based on Java applets that provides the user interface and the communication with the server. The client interface

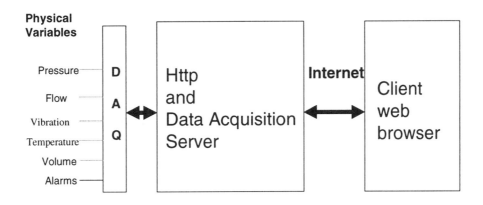

Fig. 1 Architecture of the Virtual Lab

contains the following elements:

- Analog Displays, icons representing any analog device, such as gauges, thermometer, etc.

- Digital Displays, icons that display the information using digital indicators.

- Control Buttons, representing Boolean controls that the user can click to send control signals to the sensor or instrument of control.

- Alarms: indicators of alarm conditions at the remote entity that will start blinking if the variable reaches a value outside the predefined range.

- Historic graphs, that is, graphics windows to show the history of the signal acquisition during a selected period of time.

- Statistics windows containing the statistics of the acquisition represented by histograms.

3. The Design

The following context diagram represents the different processes, inputs and outputs of the **Virtual Lab System** (Fig. 2). A description of the different components is as follows:

- *Inputs,* provided by the instrument and control devices and by the user through the client or server interfaces.

- *Outputs*, control signals to the sensors or instruments and the acquisition data, displayed in the Web browser.

- *Server processes,* that perform data acquisition and control of the sensors or instruments, transmit data, receive parameters of control, translate the data to HTML format and verify password.

- *Client processes,* that get input from user, send/receive data to/from server get the parameter of control from the user, and display data.

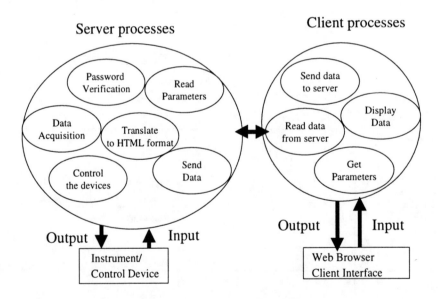

Fig. 2 Context Diagram of the Virtual Lab

Regarding the communication between client and server processes, we investigated three basics ways that are described below:

3.1 First Approach: Sockets

In this approach (Fig. 3), the data acquisition program gets the values of the physical variables. A server communication program requests the data from the acquisition program and sends them to the client. Sockets are used to communicate the server with the client. The client program contains a Java applet that display the data. The advantage of this approach is that both the server and client programs are implemented in Java. The system does not require a proprietary server to communicate the data. The only proprietary piece of software is the acquisition program that is necessary to read the values of the external devices.

The disadvantage is the requirement to implement in the server communication program a routine that calls the API (application programming interface) of the acquisition program to get the input data. Not all the acquisitions drivers provide such APIs. Sometimes, the API routine requires specialized software.

3.2 Second Approach: HTTP and CGI

In this approach (Fig. 3), an HTTP server is used to transfer the information from the data acquisition program to the Java applet client, which receives the data in an HTML format and displays it graphically.

The Java applet, also, can send control parameters to the HTTP server using CGI commands. These control parameters are then processed and handed to the data acquisition program, which transfers them to the instrument and control devices.

The advantage of this approach is that it follows the conventional Internet model of transfer of information. The disadvantage is that the HTTP protocol is a stateless protocol that was not designed to maintain continuous communication with a client. The design goal was to service the request for information of multiple clients. This is a limitation to monitor or control physical variables in real time. Another limitation is that the user of the system must develop both the CGI program and the Java applets.

3.3 Third Approach: Real-Time Protocol

In this case, a dedicated server based on the Real-Time Protocol [7] specification is used (Fig.3). The real-time server can spawn a plug-in in the client browser. The plug-in becomes the user interface for the acquisition and control of variables.

The advantage of this approach is that it allows establishing continuous connection and the delivery of real time data. This approach is similar to the one used by real-time multimedia applications such as Real Audio and Real Video. The disadvantage is that there is no real time server based on the RTP protocol for data acquisition and control of variables. The implementation of this kind of server is still a matter of further development.

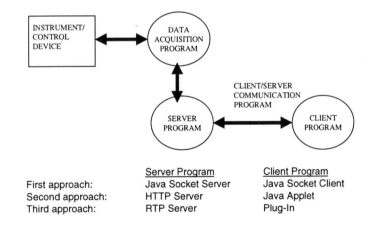

Fig. 3. Three Approaches for
Client/Server Communication

4. Implementation

A prototype was implemented to demonstrate the viability of conducting remote experimentation through the Internet. A simple virtual lab assignment was designed. The user will monitor remotely the current value of temperature and generate alarms when the temperature is outside of a predefined range. The system runs using a Labview server under Windows NT/95 and Web browser as the remote client.

The Figure 4 shows the sequence of actions to display the current value of the temperature. The data acquisition program reads the temperature from the sensor and sends the data to the HTTP server, which waits for requests by the client. The client programs request the data, wait for the answer and display the received data in the browser.

The state diagram for the alarms (Fig. 5) shows the following sequence of events. The client program waits for alarm commands. When the user activates the alarm the request is sent to the HTTP server, which transfer the data to a CGI program. The CGI program parses the user input and sends the information to the acquisition program, which sends the control signal to the digital output to activate the alarms selected by the user. Finally, the current state of the alarms is displayed in the client interface.

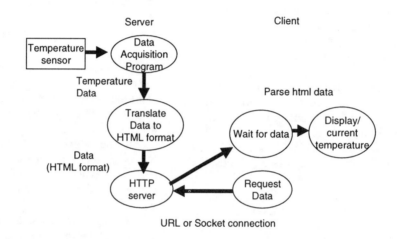

Fig. 4. Sequence of Events for Temperature Acquisition

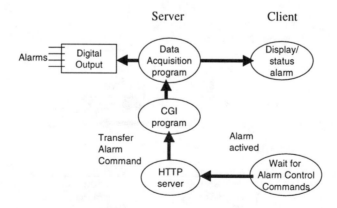

Fig. 5. Sequence of Events for Alarm Control

84

5. Conclusion

The concept of a Virtual Lab is very attractive as an educational tool. This project has been successful in showing the viability of creating virtual lab assignments to conduct remote experimentation through the Internet. However, the Virtual Lab requires improvements. A more complete set of Java applets must be developed to display more information about the variable that are being monitored and controlled. Further work is needed to the train of faculty members interested in using the Virtual Lab in their classes.

References

[1] http://www.usc.edu/dept/raiders

[2] http://www.natinst.com/daq/weather

[3] http://www.ida.liu.se/~her/npp/demo.html

[4] http://www.ece.cmu.edu/afs/ece/usr/stancil/ web/virtual-lab/virtual-lab.html

[5] http://www.ece.orst.edu/~aktanb/IEEEpaper.

[6] Carnegie Mellon University. Virtual Lab Homepage http://www.ece.cmu.edu/afs/ece/usr/stancil/web/virtual -lab/virtual-lab.html.

[7] RTP: A transport Protocol for Real-Time Applications IETF Draft, November 20, 1995.

A VESL for Real-Time Computing in an Undergraduate Computer Engineering Program

Matt W. Mutka[†] and Diane T. Rover[‡]
[†]Department of Computer Science and [‡]Department of Electrical Engineering
Michigan State University
East Lansing, MI 48824

Abstract

Embedded computer systems play an increasingly important role in today's society. Such diverse technologies as avionics, automobile drive trains, communication systems, and medical equipment are relying on computers to control system parameters. To adequately prepare today's computer science, computer engineering, and electrical engineering students for their future careers, the special problems with embedded systems development, which includes real-time system development, must be adequately addressed in their education. To meet this challenge, we are beginning the VESL (Visions for Embedded Systems Laboratory) Project. Among its goals, it proposes to provide students with hands-on, real-world experiences in embedded computer system development in an active, collaborative learning environment. Real-time system design constraints, which include the analysis of the scheduling feasibility of a system, will be studied from the very beginning of the laboratory project designs.

1 Introduction

Embedded computer systems play an increasingly important role in today's society. Such diverse technologies as avionics, automobile drive trains, communication systems, and medical equipment are relying on computers to control system parameters. Although embedded computers are powerful and flexible tools for industry, these very advantages have contributed to a corresponding increase in system complexity. Traditional approaches to system development have not successfully handled the problems of increased system complexity. Ironically, it is becoming clear that the powerful control logic that embedded computers bring to a system can also impair the ability of the systems analyst to study and understand, and hence control, the system's behavior. To adequately prepare today's computer science, computer engineering, and electrical engineering students for their future careers, the special problems with embedded systems development, which includes study of real-time system development, must be adequately addressed in their education.

To meet this challenge, the VESL (Visions for Embedded Systems Laboratory) Project addresses three needs in undergraduate computer science and engineering education: (1) provide students with hands-on, real-world experiences in embedded computer system development in an active, collaborative learning environment, which includes the transfer of real-time computing principles to undergraduate computer engineering students [1, 2, 3, 4]; (2) increase accessibility of specialized laboratories to students to allow different learning paces and approaches and to support different contexts and types of interaction; (3) share costly laboratory resources with other universities [5].

The VESL Project is undertaken at Michigan State University within the Departments of Electrical Engineering and Computer Science and in collaboration with three smaller universities in the State of Michigan: Lake Superior State University, Grand Valley State University, and Saginaw Valley State University. These universities represent several types of engineering programs

86

(from an electrical/computer engineering technology program to an electrical engineering program) which include an embedded system design component. The VESL name highlights an important aspect of the curriculum development: use of laboratories to support integration of material throughout a student's program. Moreover, the name is symbolic of the connective and open features of the proposed laboratory. It will support connective learning, facilitating closer interaction among students and instructor. It will connect students with real systems and real problems. It will be open to students on and off campus via the Internet, so that "open" takes on an extended meaning encompassing accessibility, networked/interoperable systems, distance education, and resource sharing. Finally, it holds a rich and diverse set of instructional opportunities in computer science and engineering.

The focus for the curriculum development is embedded computing systems. Research results in real-time computing, software engineering, and wireless systems are transferred to the instructional domain. We are applying a concept-driven, modular development approach that is called *"Open Your I's"* (to active learning). The premise of the approach is that concepts are learned by a process of *Introduction, Instruction, Illustration, Investigation*, and *Implementation*. The development of "I" modules will facilitate integration across the curriculum, including cross-pollination of subject matter, as well as dissemination to other universities. Additionally, it provides a structured means to transfer techniques and tools from research into instruction. The lab will facilitate curriculum innovations from introductory courses through senior design project courses; in the former, it will be used for demonstration and case study purposes, while in the latter, for hands-on design. In the lab, a station is equipped to support embedded, real-time software development, hardware design, and system testing. An array of laboratory experiences, including a radio-controlled cars project and industry-sponsored projects, are being developed and coordinated to introduce the students to a variety of contemporary, challenging issues.

2 VESL Example

We are constructing an environment in which radio-controlled (toy) cars are "driven" by computer programs constructed by the students. Each controlling computer has an interface card that emits radio signals to move and direct a car. The model cars are of the quality that one finds at typical toy stores and regularly used by young people. The software developed by the students guides the car along a path within the laboratory. Obstacles for the cars are placed along the path of the cars. Video cameras are positioned in the room and provide visual display of the path to a computer monitor used by the student. The student at the monitor may be located within the laboratory, or remotely (via the Internet), to view the cars in the path.

A student project based upon autonomous or radio-controlled vehicles is not new [6]. It has been developed in various forms at academic institutions ranging from MIT and the University of Illinois to the University of South Carolina, New Mexico State University, and Iowa State University. Additionally, it has been used for various student competitions, including one in mid-Michigan called "Bucket of Parts." We have first-hand experience with such projects, for example, using an off-the-shelf radio-controlled car (Team Associated RC10) and Polaroid ultrasonic sensors [7]. From the literature and our experience, it is clear that this type of project has considerable pedagogical value. Our goal is to leverage off of this project both in introductory and design courses so as to provide students with experience in new embedded computing and wireless communication technologies. Students apply real-time computing principles to understand the feasibility of the constraints of the computing tasks they develop.

Learning is enhanced by vehicle races, obstacle maneuvers, and other activities by the students in our laboratory. Fundamental operating system concepts such as synchronization and advanced concepts in distributed computing and communications are given practical application. The students become acquainted with equipment that is part of the future paradigm of mobile, wireless, and ubiquitous computing.

3 Open Your I's

Curriculum development in the project focuses on active teaching and learning. To support this focus, an innovative concept developed by one of the authors for active reinforcement is chosen. For the students, the design courses **open your I's**. The **I's** that are opened are *Introduction, Instruction, Illustration, Investigation,* and *Implementation.*

For example, consider the use of modules in which a radio-controlled (toy) car setup will introduce advanced issues. "I" Modules are not dependent upon a laboratory; however, this example shows how a laboratory can play varying roles in different modules. The course begins with an *introduction* module, in which the ubiquitous computing paradigm is introduced and motivated. The setting for the paradigm is given. Students are required to conduct exercises in which they detail applications in business, science, medicine, and other disciplines in which ubiquitous computing will apply. A project paper details their ideas, which includes background literature surveys by the students.

An *instruction* module follows with technical discussions of the capabilities of wireless technologies. Instruction is given regarding the bandwidth capacities and transmission quality of various wireless networks. General issues regarding mobile and nomadic computing are discussed. Compression technologies for multimedia are presented. A survey of devices that are components of ubiquitous computing environments are studied. In addition, instruction is given regarding the power requirements and constraints of the devices. An introduction to real-time scheduling algorithms is given.

Illustration of the problem to be solved in the lab by the students is conducted in the next module. Presentations of a computer controlled mobile toy car environment are given. The presentation may be in the form of a live demonstration of the environment. Previously prepared video of the environment is shown to the class to describe the issues to be explored and the problems to be solved. Individuals are assigned to teams to develop control and vehicle location software components, initiating the *investigation*. Other individuals will be responsible for developing testing and performance components. Design teams are instructed to develop both distributed and centralized algorithms for control and location discovery. Fault diagnosis and sensor calibration are needed. The feasibility of the real-time constraints are considered from the very first phases of the designs. Tools such as DRMS [4] will aid the students with this analysis.

After the specifications of the designs of the systems by the teams are developed, then the *implementation* module is planned. In the implementation, the designs are developed for the laboratory hardware. Designs are developed using the simulation and emulation tools in the laboratory. As designs are ready for testing, then the implementations control the physical devices of the laboratory. Performance, correctness, and fault-tolerance of implementations are evaluated.

Each module reinforces key design issues and concepts. The laboratory may be exploited to the extent possible in all the modules in the course, from an introduction module through an implementation module.

The use of instructional modules not only forms bridges within courses but also between courses. Significant relationships among modules will be explicitly specified as part of the curriculum development. We also recognize that students will use existing laboratory facilities in some courses, in which the lab equipment may be separate and specialized. In this case, the use of related modules may unify the laboratory experiences and create additional linkages.

Acknowledgment

The VESL project is only beginning. A prototype offering of a laboratory design course will be given in the Summer, 1997 [8]. As curricular and laboratory developments proceed, course materials will be disseminated via the VESL web site. The authors wish to acknowledge current members of the VESL team, which include Betty Cheng and Chin-Long Wey of Michigan State University, Alan Niemi of Lake Superior State University, and Tirumale Ramesh of Saginaw Valley State University. The VESL Project is supported by the National Science Foundation as part of the CRCD Program under grant number EEC-9700732.

References

[1] D. Gajski, F. Vahid, S. Narayan, and J. Gong, *Specification and Design of Embedded Systems*, Prentice Hall, 1994.

[2] G. De Micheli and R. Gupta, "Hardware/Software Co-Design," *Proceedings of the IEEE*, 85(3), March 1997, pp. 349-365.

[3] W. Campbell and K. Smith, editors, *New Paradigms for College Teaching*, Interaction Book Company, 1997.

[4] M. W. Mutka and J.-P. Li, "A Tool for Allocating Periodic Real-Time Tasks to a Set of Processors," *Journal of Systems and Software*, vol. 29, pp. 135-148, 1995.

[5] A. Speicher et al., "ASEE Project Report: Engineering Education for a Changing World," *ASEE PRISM*, December 1994.

[6] J. Byrd and J. Hudgins, "Teaming in the Design Laboratory," *ASEE Journal of Engineering Education*, 84(4), October 1995, pp. 335-341.

[7] Alviar, A., "EE 490: Embedded Systems Project," Report, Michigan State University, Summer 1996.

[8] D. Rover and P.D. Fisher, "Cross-Functional Teaming in a Capstone Engineering Design Course," submitted for publication, Michigan State University, March 1997.

Creation of the Laboratory for Fieldbus-based Automation Systems

Zdeněk Hanzálek
Trnka Laboratory for Automatic Control, DCE
Czech Technical University in Prague, Czech Republic
hanzalek@rtime.felk.cvut.cz

Emilia Schmieder and Peter Wenzel
FZI, Forschungszentrum Informatik Karlsruhe, Germany
schmieder@fzi.de, wenzel@fzi.de

Abstract

In the area of distributed control systems (DCS) a systematic design of a modular control system and reliable communication support are of major importance. This paper presents a field level of automation systems and its real time factors. A DCS is supposed to be real time capable if both application and communication as two qualitatively different sub-systems meet the real time requirements. The real time capability of the communication part of automation components is determined by the fieldbus protocol specification and its implementation. Therefore training in this type of know-how should be regarded as an integration process of several related areas. Since this knowledge has an applied character, the best effect can be achieved when the training process is closely connected with direct practical experience. A multi-national effort to create a RTS teaching/learning program brings new perspectives to a foundation of competence centers equipped with necessary technologies.

1 Introduction

A student's first encounter with the issue of concurrent behavior of systems is usually in an operating systems course. In an operating systems course the topic is usually discussed in a context of a multitasking environment where several tasks communicate with each other. This approach is then adopted to the multiprocessing systems. In the area of control we are often coping with problems of decentralized control systems. In such environment a systematic design of a flexible and modular control system and reliable communication support [1] are of major importance. Conventional industrial systems have already been in the process of being replaced by distributed intelligent systems, where intelligence is increasingly being located in the process area of such systems. Nearest to the process is the field area of an industrial system, which connects the control area with the production process itself [4]. When analysing the communication means on the different factory automation levels, it becomes obvious that the real time requirements get more critical when approaching the physical process. The fieldbus is the communication medium which has a most direct interface to the technical process.

2 Field level of automation systems

The variety of existing fieldbus standards is large due to the different requirements of their application areas [7]. One of the most important representatives among the available standards is the PROFIBUS, issued in Germany (EN 50170, 1996) [2]. Its architecture is based on the ISO/OSI layer model. PROFIBUS is designated for connecting highly decentralized process controllers with smart input/output devices. In these applications industrial controllers communicate over rapid cyclic communication connections with simple input/output devices. The focus here is set on the transmission data rate and hence on the relative simpler communication rules. The bus access methods enable a strict and deterministic observance of the real time requirements. The safe data transmission is ensured by the coding rules of the protocol data units, by connection control and retries of transmitted data. The specified communication mechanism enables an application in a real time environment.

The prevailable automation components in the field and control levels of the automation hierarchy are the process controllers and field devices. In the terms of a communication system they are regarded as nodes. Examples of process control devices are PLCs, NCs, RCs and industrial PCs. With regard to the internal operating system [3, 5], for example, the PLCs and

90

the industrial PCs differ considerably. The PLCs run their programs in a cycle, while the industrial PCs usually contain a priority oriented real time execution system. From the communication point of view the devices do not differ from each other.

Field devices differentiate from application viewpoint stronger than control devices. Examples for field devices are digital and analog I/O devices, frequency and voltage converters, valve drivers and measuring transducers. The great variety of field devices is due not only to the various application processes but also to the differences regarding the complexity and performance between the field devices. Their communication part however is identical. In terms of PROFIBUS they behave as slaves on the bus.

3 Real time factors on the field level

The real time requirements in general are determined by the characteristics of the controlled technical process. A distributed automation system is real time capable if both application and communication as two qualitatively different sub-systems meet the real time requirements.

The real time capability of the communication part of automation components is determined by the fieldbus protocol specification and its implementation. It includes two aspects. First, each component of the system has to be real time capable. Second, the specified synchronization mechanisms and medium access methods have to guarantee a real time capability of the whole system. E.g., a single component has to be able to react on requests or convert data in process values quick enough. A multi master system e.g., has to grant the bus to a master within a defined time interval.

An experimental laboratory aimed to teach real time factors on the field level should be equipped with a complex physical model able to demonstrate the following aspects:

- The real time criteria and parameters are determined by the technical process.

- The real time characteristics of the control units is mainly determined by the task scheduling system.

- The real time capability of an application is determined by its component hardware architecture and the performance of the processors used.

In order to estimate if an automation system is able to control a technical process, two considerations have to be made. On one hand, the elapsed time which the automation system needs to cause a reaction on

the technical process after an event on the technical process level has occurred should be determined (see Fig. 1, upper part). On the other hand, it has to be defined how much time it takes to evaluate if a control action has been carried out successfully (see Fig. 1 lower part).

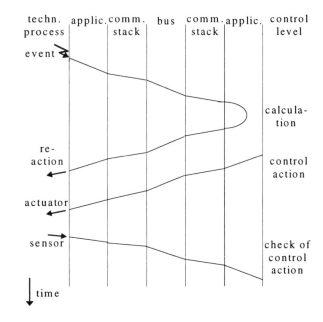

Figure 1: Phasing of control flow in automation systems between field and control level

In the separate phases the following specific time values are estimated:

- application on technical process side (field devices): time for transformation of physical quantities of the technical process into digital data and vice versa, and time for a local process control if an intelligent device is used

- application on control level side: time the application program and operating system need to initiate and check control actions and to react to events from the technical process, and time to check sensor values and supply actuators with new data

- communication stack: time the communication software needs to supply the digitalized process data (from the technical process or the control unit) in order to transmit it over the bus, and to pass the received data to the application program of the control unit or to convert the received data into process quantities

- bus: time the bus control system needs to transmit data from one node to another, time of transmission on physical layer (source and destination hardware, bus line)

The ratio between the time durations of the different phases varies in a wide range. In some cases the transmission time on the bus is long in relation to the time the application of the control units requires. This occurs mainly at multi master automation systems with long bus lines, where the data transmission rate is small, e.g. in building automation. In other cases application programs need much more time than the transmission over the bus. It usually happens in a production cell where a robot is controlled by a mono master fieldbus architecture with a high transmission rate.

4   Teaching fieldbus based automation

From the above outline it becomes obvious that the fieldbus technology is relatively complex and requires knowledge in different areas: control of technical processes, distributed systems, application and software design, hardware, operating systems, communication technology, etc. Therefore training in this type of know-how should be regarded as an integration process of several related areas. Since this knowledge has an applied character, the best effect can be achieved when the training process is closely connected with direct practical experience (see Figure 2). The foundation of competence centers equipped with the necessary technology is a basic prerequisite for practical application and testing of the acquired knowledge. Furthermore such a center becomes a test field for introducing the latest achievements of the fieldbus technology or experimenting with own know-how, thus being always up to date with the newest development trends.

Undergraduate students participate in all stages of the multi-vendor pilot system development: testing of the single devices, configurating and integrating them into a whole system, adjusting of the communication parameters, diagnostics and maintenance of the already functioning application. The existing pilot systems (PROFIBUS) will be extended by other field buses (CAN, FIP, ...) [6, 7], thus making possible to gain expert knowledge for making a comparative analysis between different field buses for finding the most favourable solution for the design of a concrete automation system. Another important result of this know-how will be the creation of hybrid field communication systems in which very simple process areas are controlled by low cost sensor/actuator buses.

Figure 2: A good demonstrator environment is important for student's motivation

5   Future work

The teaching and learning programme involves three universities from Germany, Switzerland and Austria having already deep knowledge of PROFIBUS technology and three universities from Poland, Hungary and the Czech Republic aiming to create the competence centres and extend their curricula in the field of fieldbus technology (for recent information see http://novell.felk.cvut.cz/traficc/). These universities are joined in a project TRAFICC which addresses the problem of the lack of teaching material to cover courses in the area of distributed real time control.

As a first activity of the technology transfer, the researchers will be trained in order to become experts. The acquired knowledge is a necessary basis for all other project activities. Then, three demonstrators, covering the different automation areas: machine automation, medical automation and robot based flexible production, will be built up. This takes place during the phases specification, construction and evaluation of the demonstrators. Each of the systems should have multivendor capability, which means that products of various companies are successfully integrated in one system. They will be designed considering the specific industrial characteristics and conditions, reflecting the specific situation of the related industry. The described activities will be reached in a close cooperation between the participants and are the first step of the technology transfer. The second transfer step deals with the initiation of the fieldbus technology transfer to industry.

Acknowledgments

This work was supported by INCO COPERNICUS Project TRAFICC and the Ministry of Education of the Czech Republic under Project VS97/034.

References

[1] G.Agrawal, B.Chen, W.Zhao, "Guaranteeing Synchronous Messages Deadlines with the Timed Token Medium Access Control Protocol", *IEEE Transactions on Computers*, Vol. 43, No. 3, 1994, pp. 327-339.

[2] *DIN 19245 Part 1&2: Process Field Buss*, Profibus Nutzerorganisation, Wesseling, 1991 (the German language original is available from Beuth Verlag, Berlin).

[3] C.Liu, J.Layland, "Scheduling Algorithms for Multiprogramming in a Hard Real-Time Environment", *Journal of ACM*, Vol. 29, 1973, pp. 46-61.

[4] N. Malcolm, W. Zhao, "Hard Real-Time Communication in Multiple-Access Networks", *The Journal of Real-Time Systems*, Vol. 8, 1995, pp. 35-77.

[5] P.Raja, G.Noubir, "Static and Dynamic Pooling Mechanisms for Fieldbus Networks", *Operating Systems Review*, ACM Press, 27(3), 1993, pp. 34-45.

[6] K.Tindell, H.Hansson, A.Wellings, "Analysing Real-Time Communications: Controller Area Network (CAN)", *IEEE RTSS'94*, S.Juan, 1994, pp. 259-263.

[7] F.Vasques, *On the integration of scheduling and communication mechanisms in the MAC sub-layer of real-time local area networks (in French)*, PhD thesis, LAAS CNRS Toulouse, 1996.

Chapter 4

Teaching Formal Methods for Real-Time Systems

Graduate Course:
Reactive and Real-Time Systems

Gilad Koren
Computer Science Institute
Bar-Ilan University
Ramat-Gan, 52900 Israel
e-mail:koren@cs.biu.ac.il
and
Natanya Academic College
Natanya, Israel

Shmuel Tyszberowicz
Computer Science Department
Tel Aviv University
Tel-Aviv 69978 Israel
e-mail:tyshbe@math.tau.ac.il
and
Academic College of Tel-Aviv-Yaffo
Tel-Aviv, Israel

Abstract

This article describes a graduate course on the subject of "Reactive and Real-Time Systems", which serves as the basis for courses taught by the authors at Bar-Ilan University and at Tel-Aviv University, and undergraduate course at the Netania Academic College and The Academic College of Tel-Aviv-Yaffo.

The course focuses on the development of provably correct reactive or real-time systems. It is mainly a theoretical course, hence the students do not build (even the simplest) systems. Still, we try to make things as tangible as possible. This means that all the mathematical and logical frameworks introduced are followed by presentation of software tools that implement them.

This course is planned so that no purchasing of special hardware and/or software is needed. All the software tools used are freely available from various Internet sites and can be installed quite easily. This should make our course attractive to institutions and instructors for which purchasing and maintaining a special lab is not feasible for budget, space or time limitations (as in our case).

1 Introduction

Reactive and real-time systems involve concurrency, have strict time requirements, must be reliable, and involve software and hardware components [21].

Reactive systems, and particularly real-time computing, have become an important discipline of Computer Science. Though most would agree the subject matter is interesting and important, little consensus exists on what exactly the syllabus should include.

1.1 Reactive Systems

Reactive systems are computer systems that continuously react to their physical environment, at a speed determined by the environment. This class of systems has been introduced to distinguish them from *transformational systems* (input, process, output).

Reactive systems include, among others, telephones, communication networks, computer operating systems, man-machine interfaces, etc. Industrial process control systems, transportation control and supervision systems, signal processing systems, etc., are examples of reactive system that also have strict timing constraints.

1.2 Real-Time Systems

Real-Time Systems (RTSs) have reactive behavior. An RTS involves control of one or more physical devices with essential timing requirements. *The correctness of an RTS depends both on the time in which computations are performed as well as the logical correctness of the results.* Many day-to-day gadgets embed relatively simple real-time systems; other RTSs are among the most complex systems being built today. The requirements range from intricacies of interfaces to providing guarantees of safety and reliability of operation. Severe consequences may result if the requirements of a system are not satisfied. Many RTSs are special purpose systems, require a high degree of fault tolerance, and are embedded in larger systems. Typically, an RTS consists

Week		Topic
Num	Duration	
1	1w	INTRODUCTION
2	3w	SCHEDULING
		Static versus dynamic scheduling; earliest deadline first
		Fixed priority scheduling for periodic systems: rate monotonic priority scheduling and deadline monotonic
		The synchronization problem: priority inheritance and priority ceiling protocols
		Surveys
5	1w	REAL TIME OPERATING SYSTEMS
6		REAL TIME REQUIREMENTS SPECIFICATION
	0.5w	Informal methods
		RTSAD
	2.5w	Formal methods
		Logics and models of real-time
		Real-time automatons (transition model)
		Temporal Logic for RTSs
9		THE SYNCHRONOUS APPROACH
	1w	General Description
	1w	Statecharts
	1w	Esterel
12	2	VERIFICATION

Figure 1: Course Outline and Schedule

of a control part and a controlled part. Examples of such systems are command and control systems, flight control systems, avionic systems, communication systems, robotics, process control systems, and more. A new expanding area of real-time computing is multimedia applications, mostly in connection with real-time communication.

1.3 Course Structure

The general structure of the course includes an introduction and a broad overview of reactive and real-time systems followed by in-depth coverage of three aspects of such systems. Our initial choice of these detailed subjects includes: *scheduling, operating systems support for real-time systems* and *the synchronous model*. We assume that an instructor using our course plan may replace one or more of these modules according to his/her preferences and the targeted audience.

In this course we demonstrate the construction of reliable systems that can be formally proven to meet their specifications; such systems are said to be *provably correct systems*. A formal framework for the specification, implementation, and verification of (temporal) properties of reactive systems contains:

- definition of the computational model of the system (i.e. the set of behaviors that are associated with the system),

- how to specify the desired requirements (especially safety and liveness properties) of a system within the computational model,

- the language to describe the system within the model (e.g. to express the proposed implementation)

- how to automatically verify that the implementation fulfills the required properties.

Our course outline is based on this framework, and each of the topics above is presented in detail.

1.4 Course Schedule

The course itself is a one semester course, about 13 weeks of 3 hours weekly. Roughly, it is organized as follows:

- Introduction to Reactive and RT systems (Section 2.1)—1 week;

- Scheduling (Section 2.2)—3 weeks;

- Real-time operating systems (Section 2.3)—1 week;

- Requirements specifications and design (Section 2.5)—3 weeks;

- The Synchronous approach for modeling reactive systems (Section 2.5)—3 weeks;

- Verification (Section 2.6)—2 weeks.

Figure 1.3 sumerized the course structure and schedule.

1.5 Course Goals

This course focuses on aspects of specification and development of provably correct (reactive) real-time systems and approaches to real-time scheduling. After completing the course, the students should understand:

- what reactive systems are,

- what RTSs are,

- scheduling algorithms,

- operating systems support for RTS,

- models of reactive systems (e.g. fair transition systems) and RT systems (e.g. clock transition systems),

- models for developing RTSs: concepts, methods and tools for the specification, analysis and design, of real-time systems. (Note that we do not deal with the low level mechanisms that are needed at the programming stage.)

- what the *synchronous model* is and some synchronous languages,

- verification methods.

2 Detailed Course Structure

This section elaborates on the topics that are covered during the course and includes references used.

2.1 Introduction

This part includes a definition of reactive systems, real-time systems, and hard real-time systems; fundamental concepts such as timeliness and predictability; characterization of RTSs; etc. It is mainly be based on [48, pages 1–9],[47, 26].

Topics Covered

- A definition of reactive systems.

- A definition of real-time systems.

- Fundamental concepts such as timeliness and predictability.

- A characterization of RTSs; typical examples of such systems. Terms such as size, complexity, reliability, safety, faults, fault tolerance, exception handling, error recovery.

- Time critical activities, non time-critical activities (hard vs. soft RTSs).

- Processes, tasks, concurrency.

- Common misconceptions (e.g. real-time is not necessarily synonymous with fast computation).

2.2 Scheduling

The scheduling of real-time computation is the phase where the final temporal properties of the computation are assigned. Schedulability analysis aims to prove whether all tasks can meet their deadlines.

In this part of the course, we classify the scheduling problems, and describe some of the approaches taken in order to fulfill the timing constraints in a (hard) real-time system. Surveys of scheduling issues can be found in [13, 11]; other references are [33, 29, 44].

Topics Covered

- Problem formulation: what's special with RT scheduling.

- *Optimal* RT schedulers for *underloaded* systems: the *Earliest Deadline First* algorithm and its optimality [34, 14]; the *Least Slack First* algorithm and its optimality [39].

- *Periodic* task models, Liu and Layland's *Rate Monotonic* priority assignment [34, 43, 31, 32]; Cyclic Executive vs. Fixed Priority Scheduling [36]; EDF scheduling of periodic systems.

- Catering for *aperiodic* and *sporadic* tasks in periodic systems [46].

- The synchronization problem: *priority inversion*, *priority inheritance* mechanism and the *Priority Ceiling protocol* [45].

- Time-triggered and off-line schedules [30].

2.3 Real-time Operating Systems

Real-time operating systems (RTOS) must enhance predictability in order to satisfy crucial real-time constraints. Hence, an RTOS warrants some characteristics which are not necessarily required in a 'conventional' operating system. Thus, for example, all delays in the system must be explicitly bounded.

In order to reduce run-time overhead, an RTOS needs to have a fast context switch, to be compact, to identify and respond to interrupts within a predefined time, and more. In addition, the kernel of an RTOS must maintain a real-time clock.

Since most modern RT systems are implemented using multitasking (and multithreading), the OS must support efficient techniques for multitasking (task creation, task communication and synchronization by means of message passing, mail boxes, queues, semaphores, event flags, signals, rendezvous, shared variables, etc.) and for task scheduling (preemption, priorities, limiting priority inversion, etc.).

We survey some commercial[1] and experimental RTOSs[2]. We explain the limitations of general purpose OSs (like UNIX, for example) for RTSs [42, 16]

2.4 RT Requirement Specification, Analysis and Design

There are many methods for the analysis and design of real-time systems.

2.4.1 Informal Methods

Gomaa [20] includes a number of (informal) methods that can be used for real-time and concurrent system design, comparing them through application to a specific common problem. Methods described include Real-time Structured Analysis and Design (RTSAD), Jackson System Development, Parnas' Naval Research Lab/Software Cost Reduction Method, Object-Oriented Design, and DARTS.

---

[1] For example, VxWorks, VRTX-32, iRMX, QNX, etc.
[2] Like SPRING, HARTOS, MARS, Real Time Mach [49, 17].

We cover one method (this year, for example, we used RTSAD). Other possible references are [15, 50, 18, 19].

2.4.2 Formal Methods

Traditionally, testing is the main method of program verification. But in large, complex systems, complete testing is not possible. Due to the nature of real-time systems, specifically the often severe consequences of failure to satisfy the requirements (for example, in safety critical systems), it is generally believed that RTSs should be specified using a formal language. Formal languages, along with additional notations and logic, enable to represent and verify temporal properties.

Topics Covered

- The need for formal methods for RTSs.

- Formal specification notations and logics like *Temporal Logic* [40, Chapter 3, pages 179–214],[37], *timed* and *clock transition model* [25, 28, 1], *Real-Time Logic* (RTL) [27], and *finite state machines*. One may choose to cover the Petri Nets formalism at this part of the course.

- Safety and liveness properties.

2.5 The Synchronous Model

Synchronous languages have been designed to ease the programming of reactive real-time systems. They also serve for the specification of the control part of an RTS. In the synchronous model, time is considered to be discrete; i.e., time scale is divided into an infinite number of non-overlapping segments. These segments are called *instants*. The synchronous hypothesis states that inputs, reaction (computation), and output—all happen in the same instant.

One of the advantages of the synchronous approach to reactive systems is that it has a clean mathematical model in which instants are considered to be points on a time scale. In other words, they provide primitives that enable a program to be considered as reacting in zero time (instantaneously) to external events.

Halbwachs [21] describes the synchronous approach and its languages.

Topics Covered

- What is the synchronous model?

- The advantages of the synchronous approach.

- Types of synchronous languages (imperative; dataflow; graphical).

- The syntax and semantics of the languages Statecharts and Esterel. Statecharts is a graphic synchronous language. Esterel is both an imperative, textual language, intended for reactive systems programming, as well as compiler which translates Esterel programs into finite-state automata.

- The fundamentals of reactive programming languages.

- Various compilation methods of synchronous languages and their respective computational models.

This part of the course is based, among others, on the following papers:

- *synchrony in general*: a general introduction to the synchronous approach [21, pages 1-6], [7], overall presentation of the synchronous technology [2].

- *Statecharts*: general description of the language [22, 23] and its semantics [24].

- *Esterel:* A general introduction [10]; the Esterel language, its semantics, and compilation methods [8, 5, 6, 41], Esterel as a process calculus, and a general discussion of preemption [4].[3]

2.6 Verification

There are two main approaches to achieve provably correct software systems. The *deductive approach* uses theorem provers to build a proven-correct system from its specification. The *algorithmic approach* uses model-checkers to verify that the system under development fulfills its specification. Both approaches need a formal specification of the system's intended behavior. Those techniques can be applied at different levels of formality and abstraction.

Our approach is to build provably correct reactive and real-time systems using symbolic model checkers. This suits our computational model well (e.g. state-machines which are the output of the compilation of Esterel programs). The formulas which specify the desired properties (requirements) of a system can be checked (by means of simulation) and can be proved (using a model checker).

Details of the software tools used for this purpose are elaborated in the following section.

3 Software Environment and Tools

To demonstrate and practice the various subjects covered in the course, we use a set of software tools. Several tools are already in use today, while others are envisioned for use by the end of the current semester. Most tools are available from the Internet. These tools include:

- The Esterel compiler.

- The Esterel Verification Environment XEVE [9]. It consists of a set of UNIX processes implementing verification functions and a graphical interface to invoke them.

- The TempEst package. TempEst [35] is a tool set for the formal verification of safety properties (expressed in Temporal Logic) of Esterel programs.

- The model checker SMV (Symbolic Model Verifier) [38]. SMV supports algorithmic verification of finite-state systems. We use a compiler for pure Esterel[4] that was developed at GMD, in St. Augustin, Germany. This compiler produces code in the SMV language.

- Tools for creating Argos specification and verification, developed at GMD [5].

We are still in the process of locating additional tools (e.g. Signal, Lustre, Modecharts, PERTS, Kronos). Figure 2 shows an example of an environment in which Esterel programs, temporal logic, and the SMV model checker are used in concert.

4 Assignments

In order to meet course requirements, the students are given several assignments that require computer usage (e.g. coding, use of software tools, etc.) as well as ones that do not (non-computer assignments). The scheduling part of the course is covered by few non-computer assignments. The students are asked to check whether a given set of tasks is schedulable using the schedulers studied.

---

[3]A complete programming example of a digital wristwatch can be found in [3].

[4]I.e., with no valued signals, no data, etc.

[5]Note that we have studied the syntax and semantics of Statecharts. We do not have the Statecharts environment available in our lab, and recently Argos tools became available by the GMD. The use of these Argos tools is not mandatory in the course. We noticed, however, that most of the students have been trying also this environment.

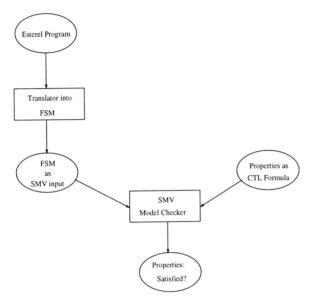

Figure 2: An Example Environment: the way a program is checked to meet its specifications

For the formal specification, design and verification parts, we provide several examples that are incrementally elaborated during the semester. We begin with an informal method to specify the system under consideration (SUC). For example, this semester we used RTSAD, hence the students used RTSA to find the processes, and Statecharts to specify their dynamic behavior.

The second assignment is given after the students have studied Temporal Logic. Here they are required to add formal safety and liveness properties to the SUC.

After the Esterel language is taught, the students implement the system using Esterel. They use Esterel's simulator to check the behavior by means of simulation. In order to formally verify that the properties that were specified by them for the SUC indeed hold, they use some of the following verification mechanisms:

- Using the GMD Esterel compiler, the source code is automatically translated into an input program for SMV. The specified assertions are added and the verification process takes place.

- In order to use TempEst, the assertions are written in a variant of Temporal Logic, and are translated into Esterel code that runs in parallel to the original Esterel program. Violation signals are emitted for each unfulfilled property.

- The XEVE environment, which locates violations of desired properties and runs a simulator that

enables to automatically replay the erroneous traces.

- We have combined the XEVE and TempEst to a unified environment.

Most recently, students' assignments included specification, analysis, implementation and verification of:

- a washing machine,

- an RFI-Lock system (a transponder-lock system with contactless key),

- an elevator system.

5 Undergraduate Course

We also teach an undergraduate version of the course. In it, the formal specification part is cut down in size and the synchronous model is presented only to the extent that problems with parallel execution of processes can be explained. The verification part is dropped altogether. On the other hand, we discuss real-time languages and devote more time to multi tasking and RTOS, as noted below. In this course we extensively use [12].

- Real-time language constructs (mainly based on Ada95)

- Real-time operating systems (Kernels)

If time permits, we also deal with the following issues:

- reliability

- fault tolerance

- hardware considerations

As can be seen, the structure of the course is similar to the format of the undergraduate course syllabus for Real-Time Systems suggested by Zalewski [51].

Acknowledgments We are grateful to Hadar Ziv for helpful comments and to an anonymous referee for constructive remarks.

References

[1] R. Alur and D. Dill. The theory of timed automata. In *REX workshop on Real-Time: Theory in Practice*, volume 600 of *Lecture Notes in Computer Science*, pages 45–73, DePlasmolen, Netherland, June 1991. Springer Verlag.

[2] A. Benveniste, G. Berry, P. Caspi, P. Couronné, F. Dupont, T. Gauthier, N. Halbwachs, P. Le Guernic, C. Le Maire, F. Mignard, J. P. Paris, and Y. Sorel. Synchronous technology for real-time systems. In *Proceedings of Real-Time Systems '94*, Paris, January 1994. North-Holland.

[3] G. Berry. Programming a digital watch in Esterel v3_2. Rapport de recherche 08/91, Centre de Mathématiques Appliquées, Ecole des Mines de Paris, Sophia-Antipolis, 1991.

[4] G. Berry. Preemption and concurrency. In *Proc. FSTTCS 93*, volume 761 of *Lecture Notes in Computer Science*, pages 72–93. Springer-Verlag, 1993.

[5] G. Berry. The constructive semantics of esterel. http://zenon.inria.fr/meije/esterel/, December 1995.

[6] G. Berry. A quick guide to esterel. http://zenon.inria.fr/meije/esterel/, February 1997.

[7] G. Berry and A. Benveniste. The synchronous approach to reactive and real-time systems. *Another Look at Real Time Programming, Proceedings of the IEEE*, 79:1270–1282, 1991.

[8] G. Berry and G. Gonthier. The Esterel synchronous programming language: Design, semantics, implementation. *Science of Computer Programming*, 19(2):87–152, 1992.

[9] A. Bouali. Xeve: An Esterel verification environment. http://cma.cma.fr/Verification/Xeve/, july 1996.

[10] F. Boussinot and R. de Simone. The Esterel language. *Another Look at Real Time Programming, Proceedings of the IEEE*, 79:1293–1304, September 1991.

[11] A. Burns. Scheduling hard real-time systems: A review. *Software Engineering Journal*, 6(3):116–128, May 1991.

[12] A. Burns and A. Wellings. *Real-time systems and their programming languages*. Addison Wesley Co. (International Computer Science Series), second edition, 1996.

[13] S.-C. Cheng and J. A. Stankovic. Scheduling algorithms for hard-real time systems—a brief survey. In J. Stankovic and K. Ramamritham, editors, *Hard Real-Time Systems*, pages 150–173. IEEE Computer Society Press, 1988.

[14] M. L. Dertouzos. Control robotics: the procedural control of physical processes. In *Proceedings IFIF Congress*, pages 807–813, 1974.

[15] M. S. Deutsch. Focusing real-time analysis on user operations. *IEEE Software*, 4(5):39–50, September 1988.

[16] B. Furht et al. *Real Time UNIX Systems*. Kluwer Academic Publishers, first edition, 1991.

[17] K. Ghosh, B. Mukherjee, and K. Schwan. A survey of real-time operating systems. Technical Report GIT-CC-93/18, College of Computing, Georgia Institute of Technology, Atlanta, georgia 30332-0280, February 1993.

[18] H. Gomaa. Software development of real-time systems. *Communications of the ACM*, 29(7):657–668, July 1986.

[19] H. Gomaa. Structuring criteria for real-time systems design. In *Proceedings of the 9th International Conference on Software Engineering*, pages 290–301, Pittsburgh, May 1989.

[20] H. Gomaa. *Software Design Methods for Concurrent and Real-Time Systems*. SEI Series in SE. Addison-Wesley, 1993.

[21] N. Halbwachs. *Synchronous Programming of Reactive Systems*. Kluwer Academic Publishers, Dordrecht, 1993.

[22] D. Harel. Statecharts: A visual formalism for complex systems. *Science of Computer Programming*, 8(3):231–274, June 1987.

[23] D. Harel. On visual formalisms. *Communications of the ACM*, 31(5):514–530, May 1988.

[24] D. Harel and A. Naamad. The Statemate Semantics of Statecharts. *ACM Transactions on Software Engineering and Methodology*, 5(4):293–333, October 1996.

[25] T. A. Henzinger, Z. Manna, and A. Pnueli. Timed transition systems. In *Real-Time: Theory in Practice, Proceedings of the REX Workshop*, volume 600 of *Lecture Notes in Computer Science*, pages 226–251, Mook, The Netherlands, June 1991. Springer-Verlag.

[26] B. Hoogeboom and W. A. Halang. The concept of time in the specification of real-time systems. In Krishna M. Kavi, editor, *Real-Time Systems—Abstraction, Languages, and Design Methods*, pages 19–38. IEEE Computer Society Press, 1988.

[27] F. Jahanian and A. Mok. Safety analysis of timing properties in real-time systems. *IEEE Transactions on Software Engineering*, 12(9):890–904, September 1986.

[28] Y. Kesten, Z. Manna, and A. Pnueli. Clocked transition systems. Stanford technical report, Department of Computer Science, 1995.

[29] M. H. Klein, J.P. Lehoczky, and R. Rajkumar. Rate monotonic analysis for real time industrial computing. *IEEE Computer*, 27(1):24–33, January 1994.

[30] H. Kopetz. Event-triggered versus time-triggered real-time systems. In *LCNS*, pages 87–101, Berlin, Germany, 1991. Springer Verlag. Proceedings of Int. Workshop on Operating Systems of the 90s and Beyond.

[31] J. P. Lehoczky, L. Sha, and Y. Ding. The rate monotonic scheduling algorithm – exact characterization and average case behavior. In *Real Time Systems Symposium*, pages 166–171. IEEE, December 1989.

[32] J. Y.-T. Leung. A new algorithm for scheduling periodic, real-time tasks. *Algorithmica*, 3(1):209–219, 1989.

[33] C.L. Liu. Fundamentals of real-time scheduling. In W. A. Halaang and A. D. Stoyenko, editors, *Real-Time Computing*. Springer-Verlag, 1994.

[34] C.L. Liu and J.W. Layland. Scheduling algorithms for multiprogramming in a hard real time environment. *Communications of the ACM*, 20(1), January 1973. SEND.

[35] C. Puchol L.J. Jagadeesan and J. Von Olnhausen. Safety property verification of Esterel programs and applications to telecommunications software. In *Proceedings the Seventh Conference on Computer-Aided Verification*, pages 290–301, Belgium, July 1995.

[36] D. C. Locke. Software architectures for hard real-time applications: Cyclic executive vs. fixed priority executives. *Real Time Systems Symposium*, 4(1):37–53, March 1992.

[37] Z. Manna and A. Pnueli. *The Temporal Logic of Reactive and Concurrent Systems: Specification*. Springer-Verlag, 1992.

[38] K.L. McMillan. The SMV system draft. Carnegie-Mellon University, 1992.

[39] A. K.-L. Mok. *Fundamental Design Problems of Distributed Systems for the Hard Real-Time Environment*. PhD thesis, Department of Electrical Engineering and Computer Science, M.I.T, Cambridge, MA, May 1983.

[40] A. Pnueli and E. Harel. Applications of temporal logic to the specification of real time systems. In M. Joseph, editor, *Symposium on Formal Techniques in Real-Time and Fault-Tolerant Systems*, volume 331 of *Lecture Notes in Computer Science*, pages 84–98. Springer-Verlag, 1988.

[41] A. Poigné and L. Holenderski. Boolean automata for implementing pure ESTEREL. Technical report, GMD, SchloßBirlinghoven, D-53754, St. Augustin, Germany, 1995.

[42] L. Salkind. UNIX for real-time control: Problems and soloutions. Robotics group,computer science department technical report no. 400, Courant Institute, NYU, New York, NY, September 1988. Appears in: John Stankovic and Krithi Ramamritham, editors. Advances in Real-Time Systems, IEEE Computer Society Press, 1992.

[43] L. Sha and J. Goodenough. Real-time scheduling theory and ADA. *IEEE Computer*, 23(4):53–62, April 1990.

[44] L. Sha, J. P. Lehoczky, J. K. Strsnider, and H. Tokuda. Logics and models of real time: A survey. In A.M. van Tilborg and G.M. Koob, editors, *Foundations of Real-Time Computing: Scheduling and Resource Management*, chapter 1, pages 1–30. Kulver Academic Publishers, 1991.

[45] L. Sha, R. Rajkumar, and J. P. Lehoczky. Priority inheritance protocols. *IEEE Transactions on Computers*, 39(9):1175–1185, September 1990.

[46] B. Sprunt, L. Sha, and J. P. Lehoczky. Aperiodic scheduling for hard real-time systems. *Real Time Systems Journal*, 1(1):27–60, 1989.

[47] J. Stankovic. Misconceptions about real-time computing. *IEEE Computer*, 21(10), October 1988.

[48] J. Stankovic and K. Ramamritham, editors. *Tutorial: Hard Real-Time Systems*. IEEE Computer Society Press, 1988.

[49] J. Stankovic and K. Ramamritham. The Spring kernel: A new paradigm for hard real-time operating systems. *IEEE Software*, 8(3), May 1991.

[50] P. T. Ward. The transformation schema: An extension of the data flow diagram to represent control and timing. *IEEE Transactions on Software Engineering*, 12(2):198–210, February 1986.

[51] J. Zalewski. Real-time systems. Undergraduated course syllabus. http://cs-www.bu.edu/ftp/IEEE-RTTC/public/, December 1993.

Introducing the Synchronous Approach into a Real-Time Course

C. André, M-A. Péraldi, J-P Rigault
Laboratoire Informatique, Signaux, Systèmes (I3S)
Université de Nice-Sophia Antipolis / CNRS
E-mail: andre@unice.fr

Abstract

This paper presents an experimental introduction of the synchronous approach in a full course in real-time system programming. This course is intended for both computer science and electrical engineering students.

The originality of the course is to combine the classical real-time programming and the new coming synchronous programming. The content of the course is given and commented. A particular attention is paid to the synchronous part, the associated software tools and environment for teaching.

1 Introduction

According to USA Today[1], in 1995, we were supposed to encounter 50 micro-controllers daily. This number is certainly far greater today. Micro-controllers are instances of "small" real-time systems. Even if *Real-Time Systems* (RTS) are so common, they are not sufficiently taught. One of the reasons is the inherent complexity of RTS. Knowledge in computer science, in automatic control, in electronics are generally demanded to deal with such systems. To make matters worse, developing a real time application requires some familiarity with the system to be monitored and/or controlled.

We have got the opportunity to teach RTS to students with different curricula: software engineering[2] or classical electrical engineering[3]. Both have a weak point: computer scientists are not especially proficient in control and electronics, whereas electrical engineering students lack programming experience. Moreover, this course addresses two different study levels: master's degree and graduate school.

Taking account of our audience and the limited amount of time available for RTS teaching, we focus on a subclass of RTS. Our main goal is to explain how a computer-based system can be efficiently used in monitoring or controlling "technical processes". The computer-based system may be a simple micro-controller, an industrial PC, or a set of processors cooperating through a real-time local area network (RTLAN).

As future engineers, our students must be given a classical background in the domain of real-time systems. A large part of the course is devoted to the classical approach to real-time systems and to "standard" industrial practice.

They must also be kept aware of new trends and perspectives. Since we are active researchers in the field of *synchronous programming*[4], we have introduced a specific teaching, including recent research results. Software tools and environments, developed for research purpose, are widely used by the students. The *synchronous approach* is not a panacea for RTS design. It is presented as a clean and elegant way of dealing with reactive systems. When control-handling aspects are predominant, this approach makes programming faster and safer, and it can lead to very efficient solutions. Thus, most of our case studies are hardware or software controllers.

At the completion of the course, students should

- have a clear vision of RTS specificities and issues,

- have gained the skills needed to develop small real-time applications, and the potential to tackle larger RTS,

- be opened to research issues.

This paper presents our proposal for a real-time course that combines classical asynchronous and recent synchronous approaches. This course has been successfully integrated into engineer and master degree curricula for three years. The main lines of the presentation are:

- a survey of the contents of the real-time system course,

- the essentials of the synchronous programming teaching,

---

[1] May 1, 1995, p 1B, quoted by Auslander[1].
[2] ESSI: École Supérieure en Sciences Informatiques, Sophia-Antipolis (F)
[3] Faculté des Sciences, Nice (F)

[4] Project SPORTS (Synchronous Programming Of Real Time Systems), Lab. I3S, Sophia Antipolis (F). See the pages on the web: http://wwwi3s.unice.fr/~map/sports.html

• the rationale for choosing the synchronous approach.

2 Contents of the RTS Course

We only give the head of chapters and some keywords. Recall that we have adopted an engineer point of view. This choice is reflected by our textbook selection.

2.1 Table of contents

1. Formal models

   • Automata,

   • Transition systems,

   • Petri Nets

2. Features of RTS

   • Temporal constraints,

   • Concurrency,

   • Predictability,

   • Dependability

3. Life cycle

   • Development cycle,

   • A semi formal specification: SA/RT

4. Classical approaches to RTS programming

   • The many ways to manage tasks cooperation,

   • Real-Time Multasking Kernel,

   • High-level languages

5. Scheduling

   • periodic/aperiodic,

   • preemptive/non-preemptive,

   • static/dynamic

6. The **Synchronous Approach**

   • (see below)

7. Distributed real-time systems

   • Computer Integrated Manufacturing (CIM),

   • Fault-Tolerant architectures,

   • Real-time local area networks: field-busses

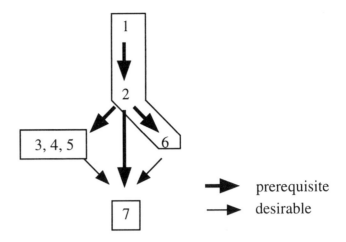

Figure 1: Precedence

2.2 References

We encourage the students to access to the general literature on RTS. The real-time system glossary and the reference library, compiled by Zalewski[5] are useful and convenient documents. For undergraduate students, we especially advise books describing an engineer approach to RTS. Their author(s) has (have) got a great experience in industrial control applications; The reader benefits from their experience. Just to mention some, we often refer to the books written by Halang & Sacha [2], Laplante [3], Bennett [4], and Labrosse [5].

2.3 Organization

This RTS course is not a monolithic block. Several teachers are involved. Chapters are distributed among three different modules. Figure 1 shows the precedence in chapters and defines the scope of each modules. A module consists of lectures, tutorials, practical sessions and laboratory work.

3 Synchronous programming course

3.1 Plan

The sections of the synchronous programming chapter are:

1. Introductory example: a mouse driver

2. The synchronous paradigm

3. A declarative synchronous language: LUSTRE

4. An imperative synchronous language: ESTEREL

---

[5] available by ftp: cs.bu.edu:/IEEE-RTTC/public

5. A graphical representation: SYNCCHARTS

6. Reactive objects

7. Formal proofs

8. Compilation of synchronous languages

9. Implementation – Execution machines

3.2 Comments

Section 1 introduces a simple *reactive system*. The goal is to detect either a single tick or a double tick on a mouse. Synchronous solutions to this problem are described in the special issue of the proceeding of the IEEE entitled *"Another Look at Real-Time Programming"* [6]. Both declarative and imperative solutions are given.

Section 2 explains and justifies the *"perfect synchrony hypothesis"* which allows the designer to abstract away reaction times. It also stresses on the advantage of having concurrency, determinism, and preemption as orthogonal concepts.

LUSTRE [7] is a functional synchronous language described in **section 3**. By several points, this language is close to temporal logics and to sequential circuits. The former aspect is appealing for computer science students. The latter makes it easier to understand LUSTRE programming for electrical engineering students.

ESTEREL [8] (**section 4**) is the oldest, and in our opinion the most representative, synchronous language. Its programming style is imperative. The kernel language, restricted to pure signals, is rather simple, and its semantics can be mathematically characterized by a score of rewriting rules. The issue of "causality cycles", for long an obscure problem for the common ESTEREL programmer, is now well-understood [9]. The different semantics of the language (behavioral, operational, electrical) are studied only in the graduate school course.

Engineers in the field of control and manufacturing systems are somewhat reluctant to synchronous languages. As a rule, they prefer *graphical approaches*. The GRAFCET [10], also known as Sequential Function Charts (SFC), is widely used in industrial programmable logic controllers. STATECHARTS [11], a hierarchical visual model which is part of the STATEMATE environment, allows the designer to program complex reactive system and it takes advantages from its industrial support. In **section 5** we introduce these models, but we focus on SYNCCHARTS. SYNCCHARTS [12] is a new graphical synchronous model that inherits from STATECHARTS, but with a better semantics (fully compatible with the ESTEREL semantics). SYNCCHARTS also supports different kinds of preemption.

Reactive objects [13, 14] introduced in **section 6**, combine reactive programming and objects. Even if some methodologies like ROOM [15] advocate the use of objects in RTS design, this promising approach needs further research and is taught only to graduate students.

Section 7 is also highly linked to research. It appears that synchronous languages, which are founded on mathematical semantics, lend themselves to formal analysis. Safety properties, which are a major concern in RTS can be formally tested (see tools below). So is the bounded responsiveness, another form of safety properties. Temporal properties are, of course, also considered.

Section 8 is reserved to computer scientists.

Section 9 is the necessary come back to the real (asynchronous) world. We describe possible architectures of *execution machines* dedicated to synchronous program execution. Studied target machines are micro-controllers [16], PC, or workstations.

3.3 Tools and software environment

For research, we have developed packages that support definition, rapid prototyping, property checking and implementation of synchronous programs. These tools, with other imported tools, are gathered in a development platform [17] used by the students.

- Input formats:
  - textual: for ESTEREL and LUSTRE programs,
  - graphical: for SFC and SYNCCHARTS

- Compilers:
  - ESTEREL and LUSTRE compilers,
  - SFC and SYNCCHARTS compilers

- Simulators:
  - XES an interactive simulator of ESTEREL programs, with visualization of the execution at the source level,
  - SFC simulation

- Connection to proof tools:
  - testing safety properties of Pure ESTEREL programs and SFC with BAC (Boolean Automaton Checker) [18] and TEMPEST [19], a temporal logic formula checker,
  - automaton and transition system analysis with AUTO [20] and MEC [21],
  - timed automata with HyTech [22]

- Execution machine implementations with various code generators.

4 Rationale for teaching the synchronous approach

4.1 Point of view

Usually, students acquire programming skills through *transformational system programming*. They are convinced that programs with never-ending loop are surely incorrect; but they do not worry about using "while statements" or recursions.

Turning to *reactive system* programming calls into question many habits. To admit that a lately delivered exact result is incorrect, is almost a revolution.

In our opinion, trying to adapt transformational programming style to reactive programming is a mistake. It seems to be better to start up in reactive or real-time programming[6] with a fresh view, and later on, to see what can be reused from classical programming.

Synchronous languages were introduced to address the issue of *reactive system* programming. As mentioned above, they bring "another look at real-time programming". We have adopted this point of view in Chapter 6 of our RTS course. Figure 1 shows that this chapter could be taught concurrently with the classical approaches. In fact, it is introduced *before*.

Besides the special issue of the proceeding of the IEEE [6], we recommend the reading of the book of N. Halbwachs entitled *"Synchronous Programming of Reactive Systems"* [23].

4.2 Main benefits

Abstraction

The synchronous approach adopts an abstract, indeed even ideal, view of real systems[7]. *Signals* are supposed to be the unique support for exchanging information. Signals are *instantaneously broadcast*: this leads to a global perception of the system. *Reactions* are generated without delay, in synchrony with stimuli.

In programming terms, the consequence is that *(internal) control takes no time*. This strong hypothesis induces drastic simplifications and makes it possible to conciliate concurrency, determinism and preemptions. Note that *preemption* must not be taken in the restricted sense given in scheduling; it is a way to ensure coordination. *"Process preemption ... consists in denying the right to work to a process,*

either permanently (abortion) or temporarily (suspension)" (G. Berry [24]).

Thanks to the "perfect synchrony hypothesis" synchronous languages have been given simple, clear, and strict semantics. This formal background explains why formal methods apply so well to synchronous programs.

Another noteworthy specificity is that synchronous programs use a *multi-form (logical) time* with a clear notion of instant. Fundamentally, a program fully defines the order of events.

Programming discipline

Due to the simplifications underlying the model, the reader may think that synchronous languages are too simple to tackle actual applications. In fact this is not the case. Other simple models like Moore or Mealy machines make it possible to design rather complex controllers. So are synchronous languages that can cope with sophisticated reactive behaviors.

Within the framework of the synchronous approach, applications are described as a set of cooperating sub-systems. Each sub-system is characterized by triggering signals and the reactions they cause. The behavior of the whole system results from the instantaneous dialogues among sub-systems.

SYNCCHARTS, which can be considered as a graphical version of ESTEREL, encourage the use of preemption for synchronization [12]. An "observer" (a sub-system) watches at another sub-system and triggers adequate reactions when special events occur. These kinds of behaviors are common in mechatronics and robotics.

Note that this approach avoids the use of communication or synchronization mechanisms such as those encountered in multitasking programming.

Application domains

We have just mentioned mechatronics and robotics. More generally, all systems with preponderant control-handling aspects can be elegantly and efficiently programmed with synchronous formalisms or languages.

ESTEREL is not restricted to this kind of application, it has also been used in protocol verification and Human-Machine Interfaces (HMI). Even if timing constraints are not stringent, the behavior of protocol and HMI may be highly reactive.

4.3 Limitations

Of course, the synchronous approach, because of its choices, has a limited scope.

First, synchronous languages have *restricted general data-processing capabilities*. Most of the data-processing

---

[6]We make a distinction between reactive and real-time. A digital filter must run within strict timing constraints and is therefore a kind of RTS, but it is not especially reactive since its behavior is not influenced by its environment. Conversely, applications like Human Machine Interfaces can be soft RTS but highly event-driven. In fact, controllers and most hard real-time applications are both reactive and real-time.

[7]See reference [12] for details.

must be supported by a host language (usually C). ESTEREL, for instance, knows about booleans, integers, and a little about strings[8]. All other data types are abstract. ESTEREL focuses on control.

The major objection is about *distributed applications*. The global perception is irrealistic, except for very special cases (synchronous LANs).

The *0-duration hypothesis* is not really a problem. Once compiled, a synchronous program has a deterministic behavior, so that you can check, a posteriori, whether or not the reactions take an amount of time negligible with respect to the time constant of the system to be controlled.

5   Conclusion

From an educational point of view, this experimental introduction of synchronous programming in a RTS course, has been very instructive.

- Starting with a synchronous language for reactive system programming has some positive effects. For students, the first contact with synchronous system programming is disconcerting because of this unusual style of programming. Indeed, they cannot establish links with the languages they know. On the one hand, this is not a flaw: students are not inclined to mimic other languages. On the other hand, they adopt quickly this new style and they are able to express non-trivial reactive behavior by the end of the first practical session.

- Such a teaching is supported by a friendly and rich programming environment. The student may experiment different input formats, execute its program (interactive simulation with backwards mapping to source), generate code for various targets.

This course is also a good opportunity to initiate student to an open and active research field. First developed in Europe, the synchronous approach is now gaining audience. The introduction of the synchronous languages in the Ptolemy environment [25] is an evidence of this evolution.

References

[1] D.M Auslander. *Mechatronics: A design and Implementation Methodology for Real Time Control Software.* not yet published, available on the web, dma@euler.me.Berkeley.edu, Berkeley (CA), 1996.

[2] W.A. Halang and K.M. Sacha. *Real-Time Systems: Implementation of Industrial Computerised Process Automation.* World Scientific, Singapore, 1992.

[3] P.A. Laplante. *Real-Time Systems: Design and Analysis, an engineer's Handbook.* IEEE Press, 1993.

[4] S. Bennett. *Real-Time Computer Control – An introduction.* System and Control Engineering. Prentice Hall, UK, 1994.

[5] J.J. Labrosse. *Embedded System Building Block.* R&D Publications, Lawrence (KS), 1995.

[6] A. Benveniste and G. Berry. Another look at real-time programming. *Proceeding of the IEEE*, 79(9):1268–1336, September 1991.

[7] P. Caspi, N. Halbwachs, D. Pilaud, and P. Raymond. The synchronous data flow programming language LUSTRE. *Proceeding of the IEEE*, 79(9):1305–1320, September 1991.

[8] F. Boussinot and R. De Simone. The ESTEREL language. *Proceeding of the IEEE*, 79(9):1293–1304, September 1991.

[9] G. Berry. *The Constructive Semantics of pure Esterel.* not yet published, available on the web, cma.cma.fr, Sophia Antipolis (F), 1996.

[10] IEC, Genève (CH). *Preparation of Function Charts for control systems*, december 1988. International standard IEC 848.

[11] D. Harel. STATECHARTS: A visual formalism for complex systems. *Science of computer programming*, 8:231–274, 1987.

[12] C. André. Representation and analysis of reactive behaviors: A synchronous approach. In *Computational Engineering in Systems Applications (CESA)*, pages 19–29, Lille (F), July 1996. IEEE-SMC.

[13] F. Boussinot. *La programmation réactive. Application aux systèmes communicants.* Collection technique et scientifique des télécommunications. Masson, Raris, 1996.

[14] C. André, F. Boulanger, M.A. Péraldi, J.P. Rigault, and G. Vidal-Naquet. Objects and synchronous programming. *RAIRO–APII–JESA*, 31(3):417–432,1997.

[15] B. Selic, G. Gullekson, and P.T. Ward. *Real-Time Object-Oriented Modeling.* J. Wiley Publ., 1994.

[16] C. André and M-A. Péraldi. Predictability of a RTX2000-based implementation. *Real-Time System*, 10(3):223–244, May 1996.

---

[8] float is to be supported by the next release of the compiler (esterel v5.10).

[17] C. André, H. Boufaïed, D. Gaffé and J.P. Marmorat. Environnement pour la programmation synchrone des systèmes réactifs. In *Real-Time & Embedded Systems (RTS&ES'96)*, pages 27–41, Paris (France), Janvier 1996. teknea.

[18] N. Halbwachs. BAC: A boolean automaton checker. Technical report, VERIMAG, Montbonnot (France), February 1994.

[19] Lalita J. Jagadeesan, Carlos Puchol, and James Von Olnhausen. Safety property verification of esterel programs and applications to telecommunication software. Liege, Belgium, July 1995. Conference on Computer Aided Verification (CAV'95).

[20] R. de Simone and D. Vergamini. Aboard AUTO. Technical Report 111, INRIA, October 1989.

[21] A. Arnold, D. Begay, and P. Crubillé. *Construction and Analysis of Transition Systems with* MEC, volume 3 of *AMAST Series in Computing*. World Scientific, Singapore, 1994.

[22] T. Henzinger, P.-H. Ho, and H. Wong-Toi. A user guide to hytech. Technical Report CSD-TR-95-1532, Department of Computer Science, Cornell University, 1995.

[23] N. Halbwachs. *Synchronous Programming of Reactive Systems*. Kluwer Academic Publishers, Amsterdam, 1993.

[24] G. Berry. Preemption in concurrent systems. *Proc FSTTCS, Lecture notes in Computer Science*, 761:72–93, 1992.

[25] W.-T. Chang, A. Kalavade, and E.A. Lee. Effective heterogenous design and co-simulation. Lake Como (I), June 1995. NATO Advanced Study Institute Workshop on Hardware/Software codesign, NATO.

Teaching Practical Formal Modeling Techniques for Complex Systems

Robert B. France*
Department of Computer Science & Engineering
Florida Atlantic University
Boca Raton, FL-33431, USA
robert@cse.fau.edu
Phone: (561)-367-3857
Fax: (561)-367-2800

1 Introduction

Courses on FSTs are often viewed by students as mathematical courses that have little relevance to "real" software development environments. While the notations and mathematical concepts used, and the apparent lack of automated support tools, contribute significantly to this perception, another factor is the failure to relate formal methods to other, more mature, software engineering methods and processes. This failure often leads the student to the view that formal methods are radical (and less appealing) alternatives to other "more practical" (i.e., more visual and easier to comprehend) specification and modeling techniques. The negative perception is often compounded by textbooks and lecturers that marginalize formal methods.

In recent years, there has been a growing awareness of the benefits FSTs can bring to the software development process (e.g., see [10]). This has resulted in the development of a number of automated environments that support the building and analysis of formal specifications and models (e.g., see [7, 9]). These works are important in that they lay the foundation for practical methods and processes based on formal techniques. One approach to developing practical methods and processes around FSTs is to incorporate the techniques into more mature and industrially-appealing development methods and processes. Methods and processes provide contexts for the use of the FST, thus it is essential that the software engineers understand the role FSTs can play in these contexts.

At Florida Atlantic University, the *Methods Integration Research Group* (MIRG) has been carrying out research on incorporating FSTs into mature structured (including object-oriented) methods [3]. Our work is the result of an observation that formal and informal graphical modeling techniques can play complementary roles in software development. In this paper we give an overview of some of our current work in this area, and present our experiences with teaching the integrated formal/informal techniques. In section 2 we give an overview of the benefits of integrating informal and formal techniques and give an example of an integrated technique for real-time systems. In section 3 we describe our experiences with teaching integrated methods, and in section 4 we conclude with a summary of our experiences.

2 Integrating Formal and Informal Techniques

In most popular graphical structured techniques (henceforth, referred to as *informal modeling techniques* (IMTs)), the syntax of the modeling constructs is well-defined, but the underlying semantics are loosely described using a mixture of natural language and diagrams. The poorly-defined semantic bases underlying most IMTs makes it difficult to rigorously analyze the behavior captured by the models they produce. This shortcoming can significantly diminish the role IMTs can play in modeling and analyzing complex systems.

One approach to making IMTs more precise and amenable to rigorous analysis is to integrate them with suitable formal specification notations. Here, integration means providing a bridge from the IMT modeling constructs to the formal notation. Research on integrated formal/informal specification techniques indicates that formal specification techniques (FSTs) can enhance the application of less formal graphical techniques, and vice-versa (e.g., see [3]). For example, most object-oriented methods (OOMs) provide good support for the important separation of concerns principle: they allow one to develop abstract models along

---

*This work was partially funded by NSF grant CCR-9410396.

a number of different views, and provide mechanisms for breaking down abstract concepts to more detailed forms. However, most OOMs provide very little support for rigorously expressing properties, thus limiting the semantic analysis that one can carry out on the models. FSTs can be used to develop more formal notions of semantic aspects, and they provide mechanisms for rigorously analyzing the resulting models. FSTs can be used to reinforce and/or instill confidence in, and to uncover problems with the graphical OO models, and a modeler's view of the domain. On the other hand, graphical OOMs can enhance the application of FSTs by providing a means for presenting formally specified properties in a visual manner.

2.1 SA/RT and Petri Nets: An integrated modeling technique

The *Structured Analysis/Real Time* (SA/RT) method developed by Hatley and Pirbhai [8] extends the applicability of graphical Structured Analysis modeling techniques to real-time systems. A SA/RT model consists of:

Data flow diagrams (DFDs) that model the required functional behavior in terms of a network of functional entities called processes;

Process specifications (PSPECs) that informally describe processes in DFDs;

Control flow diagrams (CFDs) that model required control behavior;

Control specifications (CSPECs) that describe how control elements depicted in CFDs affect system behavior; and

Response time specifications that state constraints on the time between a stimulus and its response.

A *Requirements Dictionary* provides additional information about the system.

The SA/RT method supports the important separation of concerns principle through its ability to represent systems along different perspectives, and its strong support for building abstract models in a top-down manner. Despite these strengths, the use of the SA/RT method on complex systems is severely hampered by its dependence on informal descriptions of behavior. In this subsection we outline how this shortcoming can be addressed by using a rigorous modeling and analysis technique in conjunction with the SA/RT method.

The rigorous modeling technique we use is the Cab Net technique developed by researchers at the Politecnico di Milano [11]. A Cab Net is an executable variant of a class of high-level timed Petri Nets called ER Nets [5]. It is supported by an automated environment called *Cabernet* developed by teams from Cefriel and the Politecnico di Milano.

In an ER net, tokens are associated with data structures, and transitions are associated with predicates (defining the conditions under which transitions fire) and actions (defining the relationship between input and output places). In ER nets, actions are relational, that is, input token values do not necessarily uniquely determine output token values. An ER net transition can fire when (a subset of) its input token values satisfy its predicate. Firing results in the removal of the enabling set of input token values and the production of output tokens as specified by the transition's action. Time can also be associated with transitions and tokens in an ER Net.

A Cab Net is a strongly typed variant of ER Nets, where each place is associated with a type, and predicates and actions refer to tokens as typed parameters. In a Cab Net, actions are functional, that is, the input token values uniquely determine output token values. The operational semantics for Cab Nets allows one to simulate behavior (including aspects dependent on time) by playing the token game.

We use Cab Nets to rigorously validate, or "test", SA/RT models of required behavior. Formal prototypes of behavior captured by SA/RT models are obtained by transforming the SA/RT models to Cab Nets. The Cab Nets obtained this way are referred to as "first-cut" models. Exercising these Cab Nets provides insights into modeled behavior, and can lead to a better understanding of required behavior.

The transformation of SA/RT models to Cab Nets is carried out as follows:

1. Identify transactions in the SA/RT model. An SA/RT *transaction* is a set of all processes involved in handling a single stimulus from the environment. A Cab Net of an SA/RT model is built up from Cab Nets of SA/RT transactions.

2. Rigorously specify the data passing through and stored in the application. Data elements are algebraically defined as abstract data types. The rigorous specifications are retained in the Requirements Dictionary after analysis. For example, part of the definition of a list structure is given below:

```
TYPE List [X :: TRIV]
USES Boolean Natural
```

```
SORT list
OPERATIONS
 [] : -> list
 addelem : elt natural list -> list
 delete-elem: natural list -> list
 isin : elt list -> boolean
 getelem : natural list -> elt
 hasindex : natural list -> boolean
AXIOMS
 (predicates defining the
  operations and expressing the
  property that the natural number
  indices are unique)
END
```

In the above, $TRIV$ is a theory characterizing the *elt* sort (for more on theories and the above style of algebraic specifications see [6]).

3. Express PSPECs more rigorously. The results are formalized PSPECs of the form *Input Condition : Output Condition*. The *Input Condition* determines the sets of necessary and sufficient input values, called the *firing sets*. A firing set causes the corresponding transition to execute and produce outputs. The *Output Condition* determines the output values generated by the process when invoked with a firing set. An *Input Condition : Output Condition* statement is referred to as a *firing action*. In order to express firing actions one may need to use additional functions. These auxiliary functions must be defined in the formalized PSPEC. A partial example of a formalized PSPEC is given below (access to data on a flow, *flow*, is expressed as *flow.value*):

Validate Purchase is a process that compares an input *price* with the amount of payment entered ($PAYMENT$), and indicates whether sufficient payment has been made or not. If sufficient payment has been made, change is also calculated.

```
PSPEC Validate Purchase
 Firing Actions:
 1. price.value not= null and
    PAYMENT.value >= price.value:
     change'.value =
      PAYMENT.value - price.value and
     sufficient_payment'.value = on

 2. price.value not= null and
    Payment.value < price.value:
     sufficient_payment'.value = off
END
```

4. Using transformation rules, convert each transaction to a first-cut Cab Net. The transformation rules embody what we call the *basic behavioral*

interpretations of SA/RT constructs. This step includes the following substeps:

(a) Implement the rigorous data specifications as C++ classes (C++ is the executable base language of the Cabernet environment).

(b) Define for each transition a *transition predicate* and a *transition action*. The transition predicate determines the conditions under which a transition will fire, and the transition action specifies the effect of a transition firing. Each transition corresponds to a unique firing action defined in a formalized PSPEC. The transition predicate and transition action are expressed in C++ notation.

5. Exercise the Cab Net and modify the SA/RT and Cab Net until desired results are observed.

Exercising a Cab Net prototype of a SA/RT model can reveal the following:

- The interpretation required is not the same as that provided by the "first-cut" Cab Net. In this case, the Cab Net is modified but not necessarily the SA/RT model.

- The intended interpretation does not give the expected result, or produces an undesirable side-effect. In this case both the Cab Net and the SA/RT model require modifications.

Below we give an example of a transformation rule used to convert SA/RT models to Cab Nets:

Transforming a process that generates a control flow

To transform a process that generates a data condition (control flow) to a Cab Net structure one first needs to determine the effect the data condition will have on the system (i.e., determine the state changes it causes, and the processes it causes to be activated and deactivated). Such information can be obtained from the CSPEC. The effect is then modeled directly in the Cab Net representation of the process.

Fig. 1 shows an example of a Cab Net representation of a process (with a single firing action) that produces a data condition, c. The control flow c causes the activation of process $P1$ and the deactivation of process $P2$ when the system is in state $S1$. In a Cab Net, the state of a system is represented by a data token in a *state place* (depicted as a large rectangle). The value of the token gives the current state of the system. The state place must always have a single token in it (else

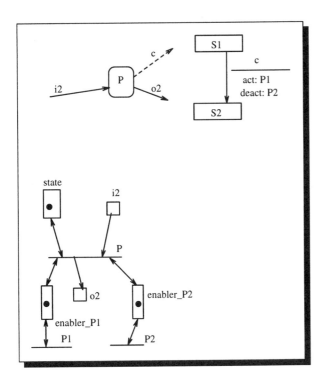

Figure 1. A Cab Net of a SA/RT process with control flows

the state will be undefined). Processes that are activated and deactivated are associated with places called *enablers* (depicted as small rectangles). Enablers must always consist of single tokens. The value of the token in an enabler determines whether the attached process is activated or not. Both enablers and state places are attached to transitions as input/output places.

The process P is modeled as a transition that is connected to a state place and two enablers (for processes $P1$ and $P2$). The enablers are also associated with $P1$ and $P2$ as input/output places.

The transition action for the process P must state, among other things, the effect of the control flow c: if the state place holds a value $S1$ then the transition updates the enablers for $P1$ and $P2$ and changes the state value to $S2$. The transition predicates for $P1$ and $P2$ must stipulate that these processes can only fire when the values in their enablers allow such firings.

3 Teaching Integrated Methods: Dispelling the Myths

We feel that it is important that students understand that FSTs are tools that can be used in the

context of practical software development methods and processes. Most software engineering textbooks treat FSTs as an isolated topic and provide very weak connections to other software engineering techniques. This does not give students the opportunity to explore useful relationships between FSTs and other tried and proven software modeling and analysis techniques. The result is that students view FSTs as radical alternatives to other modeling and analysis methods rather than as possibly complementary tools.

To address this problem, FSTs should be introduced in general software engineering courses. The FST-related materials should present FSTs in terms of their strengths, weaknesses, applicability and limitations, relative to other techniques. For example, course material should stimulate discussions on how FSTs can enhance requirements and design inspections, requirements prototyping, design simulation and animation, and systematic code testing. This is not to say that courses that focus on FSTs have no place in the curriculum. FST-specific courses are essential to developing in-depth technical FST-related skills.

A software engineering program that incorporates relevant aspects of FSTs into its development-related courses is more likely to produce students that have a good appreciation of the role FSTs can play in development. In our experiences, a significant barrier to this approach, other than the mathematical preparedness of students, is faculty resistance to exploring the application of FSTs in "non-FST" courses. We expect such resistance to diminish as awareness of the benefits of FSTs increases.

In our software engineering courses we introduce FSTs as a tool that specifically addresses the important formality and rigor principle of of software engineering. Students are taught that use of FSTs does not preclude use of other tried and proven software engineering techniques that address similar concerns. At the undergraduate level we introduce FSTs in the Principles of Software Engineering course. The course is roughly structured into four parts as follows:

1. Introduction to software engineering

   (a) Software development problems
   (b) Software engineering principles and qualities
   (c) Software development models

2. "Informal" software engineering techniques

   (a) Introduction to Structured Analysis/Design (SA/D) and Object-Oriented Analysis/Design (OOA/D).
   (b) Formal Reviews and inspections

(c) Modeling exercises

3. Rigorous software engineering techniques

   (a) Introduction to FSTs

   (b) Formalized OOA/D and SA/D techniques

   (c) Formalizing results of previous modeling exercises

4. Software quality assurance, reuse, project management

In the second part of the course the students (working in groups) model and analyze medium-sized systems using SA/D and/or OOA/D techniques. In the third part, the students return to these models and attempt to formalize them. Invariably, the formalization they carry out uncovers problems with their original models. We have also designed undergraduate project courses around our integrated methods (e.g., see [4]). Our experiences indicate that students, while they had significant problems with the mathematical notations and concepts, gained a deeper appreciation of the benefits FSTs can bring to software development.

At the graduate level, in-depth FST-skills are developed in the Rigorous Specification and Analysis course. In that course students learn how to write and analyze Z specifications [12], and are introduced to other formal specification notations (e.g., Petri Nets, algebraic specifications). We have recently added materials on the B notation to this course. In the previous offering of the Computer Aided Software Engineering course we introduced students to an integrated OO/FST technique, and required that they use the technique to model and analyze the requirements of a medium-sized system (for a description of this course see [2]). In the next offering of the course we plan to introduce students to the integrated SA/RT and Cab Net technique outlined in this paper.

We take an "active" approach to introducing FST concepts [1]: we engage students during the classes in the development of formal models. This not only keeps the students alert and awake(!), but it stimulates discussions that help us better understand and address the problems students are encountering with the course materials.

The mathematical preparedness of students affects their ability to master FST skills. We have observed that our students are not well-prepared. To address this deficiency we are currently developing remedial undergraduate and graduate materials. Ideally, students would be required to take additional mathematics courses. Making mathematics part of a program's core requires a departmental philosophy that is favourable to mathematical software development techniques. In the absence of such a philosophy, the best approach is to incorporate the remedial mathematical materials into software engineering core courses. The success of doing this is heavily dependent on the leanings of the lecturer teaching the course.

4   Conclusions

In this paper we discuss the role integrated formal/informal modeling techniques can play in developing software, and in exposing students to some of the practical benefits of FSTs. Our experiences indicate that introducing FSTs in general software engineering courses gives students a better opportunity to explore how FSTs can be used in conjunction with other software modeling and analysis techniques. The major problems we encountered in teaching FSTs relate to student preparedness and faculty indifference to these techniques. We are currently developing remedial materials to address the preparedness problems. The faculty indifference we hope will change as research and use of FSTs continue to provide evidence of the benefits that can be realized.

References

[1] C. N. Dean and M. G. Hinchey. Introducing formal methods through rôle-playing. *ACM SIGCSE Bulletin*, 27(1):302–306, Mar. 1995.

[2] R. B. France and J.-M. Bruel. The Role of Integrated Specification Techniques in Complex System Modeling and Analysis. In *Proceedings of the Workshop on Real-Time Systems Education (RTSE'96)*, Daytona Beach, Florida, 20 Apr. 1996.

[3] R. B. France, J.-M. Bruel, and M. M. Larrondo-Petrie. An Integrated Object-Oriented and Formal Modeling Environment. *To appear in the Journal of Object-Oriented Programming (JOOP)*, 1997.

[4] R. B. France and M. M. Larrondo-Petrie. Understanding the role of formal specification techniques in requirements engineering. In *Proceedings of the 8th SEI Conference on Software Engineering Education*, volume 895 of *Lecture Notes in Computer Science*, pages 207–222. Springer-Verlag, 1995.

[5] C. Ghezze, D. Mandrioli, S. Morasca, and M. Pezze. A unified high-level Petri net formalism for time critical systems. *IEEE Transactions on Software Engineering*, 17(2), 1991.

[6] J. A. Goguen and T. Winkler. *Introducing OBJ3*. SRI International, 1988.

[7] J. V. Guttag and J. J. Horning. *Larch: Languages and Tools for Formal Specification*. Springer-Verlag, New York, 1993.

[8] D. Hatley and I. Pirbhai. *Strategies for Real-Time System Specification*. Dover Press, 1987.

[9] M. Saaltink. Z and Eves. In J. E. Nicholls, editor, *Z User Workshop, York 1991*, Workshops in Computing, pages 223–242. Springer-Verlag, 1992.

[10] H. Saiedian. An Invitation to Formal Methods. *Computer*, 29(4):16–30, Apr. 1996.

[11] S. Silva. *Cabernet user manual*. CEFRIEL and Politecnico di Milano, Italy, 1 edition, May 1994.

[12] J. M. Spivey. *The Z Notation: A Reference Manual*. Prentice Hall, Englewood Cliffs, NJ, Second edition, 1992.

A COURSE ON PERFORMANCE EVALUATION OF COMPLEX

DISTRIBUTED SYSTEMS

Boleslaw Mikolajczak
Computer and Information Science Department
College of Engineering
University of Massachusetts
Dartmouth, MA 02747
bmikolajczak@umassd.edu

ABSTRACT

This paper presents an implementation of a graduate course devoted to performance evaluation of complex parallel and distributed computer systems. Novelty of the course stems from an application of a combination of two known approaches in the same course. The first approach, queuing networks theory, is classical and well described in literature. The second approach, modeling using timed and stochastic Petri nets, is also well-known as an independent way of solving performance problems for multiprocessor systems. We combine these two approaches, compare them, and show relationships and areas of potential applicability. We present the following components of the course: course syllabus, assignments, projects, lecture notes, and research components of the course in detail. The focus of this paper is on the role of Petri nets in performance evaluation of distributed systems.

1. INTRODUCTION

When designing systems correctness is a primary goal. Nowadays it is evident that performance aspect has to be included in the design process from the very beginning. For instance when Intel started development of processor P6 the main goal was to have a processor with performance twice as good as for Pentium assuming that no new technological advances will be applied. Such requirements imply that the only source of performance improvement can come from an architectural optimization. This simple example indicates that performance evaluation should be a component of any design; it should be a concurrent component of the design's optimization. We developed a course which incorporates a performance evaluation in a design process, especially for parallel and distributed systems. Timed and stochastic Petri nets are used to model and evaluate such systems. In particular, we present a performance evaluation of client-server systems from

perspective of two parameters: response time, and throughput.

2. COURSE DESCRIPTION

This is a technical elective course in the MS graduate computer science curriculum at the University of Massachusetts Dartmouth, denoted as CIS 578, Evaluation of Computer Systems Performance (ECSP). The following topics are included: performance measures of computer systems, techniques of analysis and simulation for evaluation of computer systems performance, queuing systems, Markovian processes, queuing networks, discrete simulations, timed and stochastic Petri nets and their application in evaluation of performance of parallel and distributed systems.

2.1. COURSE OBJECTIVES

To provide quantitative rules of evaluation computer systems performance both for uniprocessor and multiprocessor (shared and especially distributed memory) systems. To verify these rules for several case studies using available software tools of computer systems performance evaluation. Great GSPN (Generalized Stochastic Petri Net), Design/CPN, and UltraSAN software simulators are used to model and to simulate systems with probabilistic and time-dependent parameters. The course has a research flavor with many lectures based on current conference and journal research articles. Performance studies of both software and hardware components of computer systems are included in the contents of the course. The course has strong science component (methods and laws of performance evaluation) and strong project/lab component (practical verification of methods and laws of performance evaluation). Performance evaluation of computer systems of the near future (multi-CPU commodity chips and multiprocessor systems) are the major components of the course.

2.2. TEXTBOOKS AND JOURNAL REFERENCES

1. M. Almone Marsan, G. Balbo, G. Conte., *Performance Models of Multiprocessor Systems*, The MIT Press, Series in Computer Systems, 1986.

2. M. Almone Marsan, G. Balbo, G. Conte, S. Donatelli, G. Franceschinis, *Modeling with Generalized Stochastic Petri Nets*, Wiley & Sons, Wiley Series in Parallel Computing, 1995.

3. Raj Jain, *The Art of Computer Systems Performance Analysis, Techniques for Experimental Design, Measurement, Simulation, and Modeling*, Wiley & Sons, 1991.

4. K. Jensen, *Colored Petri Nets, Basic Concepts, Analysis Methods and Practical Use*, vol.1-1993, vol.2-1994, vol.3-1997, Springer Verlag.

5. M. K. Molloy, *Fundamentals of Performance Modeling*, Macmillan, 1989.

6. International Journal "*Performance Evaluation*", North-Holland Publishing Company.

7. Proceedings of the Workshops on Petri Nets and Performance Models (PNPM); IEEE Computer Society, since 1985.

8. *IEEE Transactions on Software Engineering*, 1989, April issue, three best papers from PNPM'87,1991, February issue, best papers from PNPM'89; special section devoted to Petri Nets as Performance models.

9. Software packages supporting performance evaluation by means of stochastic Petri nets: GreatGSPN, UltraSAN, TimeNet.

2.3. COURSE CONTENTS

Below a more detailed course contents is presented topic by topic.

WHAT IS EVALUATION OF COMPUTER PERFORMANCE?

Role of stochastic processes, operating systems and computer architecture in CSPE. Measuring vs. modeling in ECSP. High-level model description tools: queuing networks and stochastic Petri nets to model parallelism and synchronization.

PERFORMANCE MEASURES FOR COMPUTER SYSTEM MODELS:

Throughput, capacity, response time, utilization, reliability, availability, speedup, backlog; workload parameters: interarrival time, task size, I/O request rate, I/O service rate, memory size, task mix, parallelism.

FOUNDATIONS OF PERFORMANCE EVALUATION:

Markov processes, discrete-time Markov chains, continuous-time Markov chains, aggregation of states in Markov chains, semi-Markov processes, finite state machines with time annotations, Petri nets with probabilistic/stochastic and time annotations. Transform Theory: Z-transform, Laplace transform.

SIMULATION:

Generating random numbers, programming simulation (timed-based, event-based simulations), analyzing simulation results, simulation of Markovian systems.

QUEUING MODELS:

Classification of queues, system utilization, deterministic analysis of a single-server queuing system, load-dependent server, Burke's theorem, birth-death systems, non-birth-death systems, non-Markovian systems, simulation of the M/M/1 queue. Little's theorem for queuing systems: formulation with proof of correctness. How to compute average number of customers in the system knowing average amount of time spent by customers in the system. Examples of Little's theorem application. Classification of queues from ECSP point of view.

NETWORKS OF QUEUES:

The routing chain, using the routing chain, the M-->M property, local balance, solving open networks, solving closed networks, networks with multiple routing chains, Jackson queuing networks, the Chapman-Kolmogorov's theorem, Pollaczek-Khachian formula, Gordon and Newell queuing networks.

CASE STUDIES:

A simple capacity planning problem, a time sharing system, a multiprocessor analysis using Markov chains, a packet switching network, a terminal access controller model, a token ring.

MULTIPROCESSOR PERFORMANCE:

Multiprocessor speed-up and Amdahl's law, performance of interconnection networks, parallel program performance: series-parallel program structures, general acyclic random graphs as models of parallel programs, multiprocessor performance with task-graph models, supercomputer performance evaluation, The Perfect Club Benchmarks, predicting performance of parallel computations using queuing network model, analysis of crossbar multiprocessor architectures.

PETRI NET BASED PERFORMANCE MODELS:

Timed Petri nets in modeling and evaluation of multiprocessor systems, stochastic Petri nets and performance evaluation, generalized stochastic Petri nets (GSPNs), performance evaluation of asynchronous concurrent systems using Petri nets, single-bus multiprocessors with external common memory - analysis using GSPNs, multiple-bus multiprocessors with external memory - analysis using GSPNs, single-bus multiprocessors with distributed common memory (four architectures) - analysis using GSPNs, multiple-bus multiprocessors with distributed common memory - Markovian model analysis.

3. PERFORMANCE EVALUATION OF CLIENT-SERVER SYSTEMS

Practical emphasis in the course is on client-server systems and a token ring. Client-server systems are characterized briefly below from performance evaluation point of view.

Who is interested in system's performance - a system designer and a customer. Techniques to evaluate system performance include:

- **measurement** (the most accurate, possible only after implementation, expensive; typical measures of quality are: elapsed times and the service demand on idle systems)
- **simulation** (discrete-event; possible at a design stage; expensive from time point of view to get statistically significant results)
- **analytic modeling** (many designs may be evaluated; include product-form queuing network models, (semi)-Markov models, Markov reward models)

Client-server system studied in class is a distributed system of one (or more servers) and many clients, such as a set of workstations accessing a file server (database server, compute server) over a local area network, for instance token ring. The analysis of client-server systems is difficult for the two following reasons:

- various dependencies that can occur in the request arrival process at the server (in a LAN, request A from station i can receive service later than another request B from station j (j<>i) , even though A is generated before B; this is called as the *overtake condition* due to randomness of the process by which stations can gain access to the network and the fact that A can be generated when there are messages waiting to be transmitted at station i while B is generated when the queue of station j is empty - i.e. queuing requests at the server are not necessarily in the same order as clients generated these requests

- arrival process at the server depends on client workstations' behavior and the arrival processes at client workstations depend on the server's behavior.

In conclusion the product-form analysis method and other methods known in literature are inappropriate because of interdependencies of arrival processes and the overtake condition. The suggested approach includes:

- **continuous-time Markov models** that capture dependencies in the request arrival process
- **stochastic Petri nets** as a means of specification and automated generation/solution of large Markov models (however Markov models have their limitations in a form of time parameters to be exponentially distributed - this limitation can be overcome by a method of stages. Another problem is the size of the state space for Markov models - to eliminate this problem one can use the *superclient aggregation method)*;

Distributed systems modeling uses a class of generalized stochastic Petri nets called *Stochastic Reward Nets (SRNs)*. Assumptions concerning the model include:

- distributed computing system consisting of N workstations
- each machine has to get an access write to the communication medium to transmit request/reply message
- workstation does not generate a new request until it has received the reply to the previous one - main reason for this assumption is a potential dependency of new client requests based on server's response; however, local processing of a client is still permitted
- each time the server captures the access right to the network it transmits at most one reply message (it is straightforward to extend this case to a sequence of messages from server or to the case when the response is shared)
- requests are serviced in a FIFO manner; 1-persistent protocol is used, i.e. a station transmits when the channel is idle; if it is busy, the station listens until the channel is idle and then transmits immediately; if the transmitted message is involved in a collision then the station waits a random amount of time and listens to the channel again
- the service of a file server system can be divided into several suboperations (disk access, disk read/write); service is considered as a single generic operation parametrized by the service rate (the mean number

of services accomplished by the server in a unit time, in absence of contention)

- workload depends on three elements: the number of workstations, service request rates, and network traffic
- global distributed computing systems is characterized by: workload, network architecture, and access protocols
- client-server model can be considered as a general framework of a file server, database server, or a compute server.

Performance parameters include two parameters:

- mean response time
- throughput.

Difference with other known models of a token ring include:

- message interdependencies introduced by the clients-server architecture
- approximate analytic-numeric method rather than simulation is used to solve the models

Stochastic Petri Nets (SPNs) are characterized by:

- ability to model asynchronous and concurrent events
- places, transitions, input places, output places
- tokens, markings, reachable markings, reachability set, and reachability graph
- arcs, multiplicity of arcs
- enability of a transition when transition can fire
- SPNs have exponentially distributed firing times for each transition
- continuous time Markov chain - each edge has assigned a weight equal to the firing rate of the associated SPN transition
- Generalized SPNs allow transitions with zero firing time and inhibitor arcs.

A transition which has inhibitor arcs may fire only if each of its ordinary input places contains at least as many tokens as the multiplicity of the input arcs and each of its inhibitor input places contains fewer tokens than the multiplicity of the inhibitor arc. The tokens in the ordinary input places are removed as this transition fires. The tokens in the inhibitor input places remain unchanged.

Stochastic Reward Nets (SRNs) are an extension of Generalized SPNs with the following characteristics:

- associate award rates with the markings of an SPN
- generate Markov Reward Models (MRMs) that combine evaluation of performance and fault-tolerance
- include *variable multiplicity arc* that permits the removal of a marking dependent number of tokens from an input place to an output place
- include *general marking dependency* that permits the rate or probability of a transition to be a function of the number of tokens of any place in the net including its input place
- include *enabling/disabling functions* that allow the firing of a transition based on the global structure of the net.

4. ROLE OF PETRI NETS

Below we elaborate more on a part of the course syllabus which underlies role of Petri nets in performance evaluation of parallel and distributed systems.

Characterization of Petri nets in ECSP

Representation of time in Petri nets: weak and strong time semantics. Several examples of systems' modeling using timed Petri nets. Time assigned to places, transitions, and arcs. Elapse and duration times representation in Petri nets. Representation of stochastic phenomena in Petri nets. Time and event-driven simulation as a method of experimental performance evaluation. Two examples: simulation of a processor performance and hard disk performance using time and event-driven simulation.

Stochastic Petri Nets vs. Markov Chains

Ergodicity in Stochastic Petri nets. Algorithm of transformation from SPNs to a reachability tree, and to Markov Chain. The Molloy's isomorphism theorem - SPNs vs. MC. Computing steady-state distributions from MC related to SPNs. Computing average time between firing of selected transitions. Computing probability of finding a property A in a reachability tree of SPN. Generalized SPNs - a generalized SPNs with two categories of transitions: immediate and timed transitions. Elements of the GSPNs analysis. Example of transformation from SPN to Reachability Tree and to Markov Chain with calculation of stochastic parameters: steady-state distribution and average firing rate of a transition.

Colored Petri Nets and their Implementation by Design/CPN

Classification of Petri nets. Dimensions in Petri Nets: data type aspect, implementation of the probabilistic aspect, time aspect, hierarchy (abstraction) aspect. Abstract Data Types as colored tokens. Binding of transition. Transition enabling. Arc inscriptions: syntax and semantics. Declarations of data types. Elements of Standard ML. Design/CPN as a visual programming approach to parallel and distributed systems. Example of resource allocation problem with computation of reachability tree.

Timed Colored Petri Nets on Design/CPN

Relationships between timed and untimed Colored Petri Nets from behavioral point of view: occurrence sets, occurrence graphs, invariants, and simulation. Time inscriptions in places, transitions, and outgoing arcs (syntax and semantics). Kinds of delays: continuous vs. discrete, constant, interval, probability distribution. Occurrence sets for timed/untimed systems. Timed multi-sets. Methods of analysis of timed CP-nets: simulation, occurrence graphs, and invariants. Timed multi-sets. Examples of applications: embedded system specification, automatic synthesis of parallel programs.

Modeling of a Multiprocessor System Using High-Level SPNs

Assumptions about Petri net - based models of multiprocessors. Functional description level for performance purposes. Architecture of a bus-based multiprocessor with shared memory. High-level Stochastic Petri Nets. Logical modeling (discrete state spaces) and stochastic modeling (stochastic processes). A concept of a compound marking and a compound reachability tree and its relation to individual marking and reachability tree. Molloy's theorem about isomorphism between reachability tree of a High-Level SPN and Continuous Time Markov Chain (k-bounded Petri nets and finite Markov processes). Properties of the compound reachability trees.

Performance Evaluation of the Client-Server Architecture

A class of Reward Petri Nets (RPNs) - special class of SPNs. Assumptions concerning client-server architecture based on a token ring LAN. Idea of an aggregate client. Three types of super-places: server, tagged client, and an aggregate client in the approximate SRN model. Three performance parameters: average response time, throughput, and parametric sensitivity. Approximate approach to performance analysis using idea of the aggregate client. Concept of the offered load. Network

parameters having influence on performance. Differences between approximate and precise SRN models.

Precise RPN model for client-server architecture. Performance characterisitcs for approximate and precise RPN models: 93% savings in time and space and 1% loss in accuracy. Algorithm of solving SRNs by means of Markov Reward Nets (MRN). Vanishing and tangible markings. Computing the generating matrix Q of the MRN. Solving for steady-state probability using Gauss-Seidel method and SOR. How to assess the parametric sensitivity of the client-server architecture based on steady state probabilities and on the generating matrix Q?

Performance Evaluation of Communication Protocols with Design/CPN

Project - Performance evaluation using Design/CPN with timed simulation (resource allocation problem and communication protocol). CPN model of timed communication protocol: declarations of ADTs and variables; time stamps. Occurrence graph for the timed communication protocol. Timed ferry system: the CP-net model. Distributed database system - CP-net model.

Shared Memory Multiprocessors with Buses

Machine repairman model. Two stochastic parameters: processor's active time and shared memory access time. Processing power P of a multiprocessor system. Performance indices of a multiprocessor system: average delay time, average waiting time, average number of waiting processors, average cycle time. How performance indices can be computed based on P using Little's law. How to compute processing power P? Modeling of a multiprocessor system using Generalized SPNs. GSPN modeling of several bus arbitration protocols (FCFS, PS, FP). Analysis of specific cases depending on stochastic properties of processor's active time, common memory access time, and on bus arbitration protocol. Representation of three classes of stochastic distributions: exponential, hypoexponential, hyperexponential by means of Generalized SPNs.

Distributed Memory Multiprocessors

Markovian models of distributed shared memory (access with different rights and speeds by different processors). Physical and logical accessibility of memory in distributed shared memory system. Three architectures with single global bus and distributed shared memory and their GSPNs models. Four architectures with multiple buses and shared distributed memory and their GSPNs models and Markov chains.

5. COURSE PROJECTS

The main components of the course are two modeling and programming projects.

The first project, with implementation in C, summarizes students knowledge of queuing network algorithms for performance evaluation of open and closed queuing networks. Students design and code a "*Queuing Network Solver*" in a Menu-based environment, a program composed of two separate parts: for open and closed queuing networks. This project provides and excellent opportunity to integrate students' knowledge of classical performance evaluation techniques and to allow computational experiments with examples previously computed in homework assignments. Typical parameters computed are: throughput, total average system delay time, average number of customers in each queue, average delay in each queue, and utilization rates for each queue and server. As a result a methodology and technology are studied in a unified manner with a significant hands-on course component.

The second project of the course is devoted to performance modeling and evaluation using Stochastic Petri Nets. Using results of previous Master Thesis supervised by the author, students run performance experiments of different versions of client/server architectures. Mutations of the architecture include: number of client processes, number of server processes, and type of the communication medium (bus, Token Ring, and Ethernet). Two parameters are measured: average response time and utilization rates. The response time is measured for the whole client/server system as composed of client, server, and communication medium (network) with respect to single client's request. Measuring of the response time is achieved by introduction of a synchronization transition in a Stochastic Petri Net model. This transition fires when a full cycle of client's request, network access, and server's response have been completed. The firing of this transition is captured by a special timed transition attached 'in parallel' to the synchronization transition. The utilization rates are measured separately for CPUs, disks, and network. A method to compute the utilization rate of all system components is the same: an absence of Petri net token in a place representing specific medium is an indication that this resource is utilized. A ratio of time when a token is absent in this place to total time of experiment is by definition the utilization rate. During the performance modeling process by means of Stochastic Petri nets students revisit the idea of step-wise abstraction: they typically have to create two/three intermediary models of the same system to reach a satisfactory level of detail.

Students can compare results of their Petri net-based simulations with values of parameters from experiments on real client-server systems of the same type.

6. CONCLUSION

This paper presents a unified approach to performance modeling. Two methodologies have been presented in a single course: queuing network and Stochastic Petri net approach. Petri nets should be used when system has: conflict, concurrency, distributiveness, parallelism, and resource allocation features.

From course experiences it is clear that time to model systems by means of Stochastic Petri nets takes significant amount of time and efforts. Simulation times are in terms of hours and even days for models with larger number of clients and servers (using UltraSAN environment on SUNstations). Benefits of using Colored Petri nets from Design/CPN software package could not be fully utilized in projects because of limited performance evaluation capabilities of this environment. For small systems the TimeNET environment installed on a laptop provides sufficient testbed for experiments.

Research paper and oral presentation of student findings are also part of the course. At the beginning of a semester an instructor assigns to each student recent research paper devoted to performance evaluation. Student studies this paper individually, writes a term report, and makes 20 minute long oral presentation at the end of the semester in front of the class. There are two objectives of this course component: to convince students that they learned knowledge at the cutting edge of methodology and technology and to give them experience in public presentations to a professional audience.

This course has been so far implemented twice to a group of approximately ten excellent and highly motivated graduate students. Their comments in course evaluations are very highly positive.

Author Index

About the Editors

 Daniel Mossé joined the faculty of the Department of Computer Science at the University of Pittsburgh in 1992. He received his BS in Math from the University of Brasilia, Brazil, in 1985, and a MS and Ph.D. from the University of Maryland, College Park, in 1990 and 1993, respectively. His main research interest is in distributed systems, more specifically the resource allocation, multimedia, real time, and fault tolerance.

He is intensely involved in undergraduate and graduate curriculum and teaching, especially in the area of operating systems. He is currently developing instructional materials for an undergraduate course in real-time operating system principles. He is currently researching real-time fault-tolerant resource allocation, real-time communications, and leading a group in the implementation and installation of a home-grown distributed reliable multimedia system. He is also interested in hypermedia system specification and presentation, visualization, and user interfaces.

Funding for these projects is provided by NSF and DARPA.

 Janusz Zalewski is an associate professor at the Department of Electrical and Computer Engineering, University of Central Florida, Orlando, Florida. Before taking a university position, he worked at various nuclear research institutions, including the Superconducting Super Collider (SSC), Dallas Texas, and Lawrence Livermore National Laboratory, Livermore, California. His research interests include real-time multiprocessor systems, safety-related computer systems, and computer science/engineering education.

Zalewski received a MSc in electronic engineering and a Ph.D. in computer science from Warsaw University of Technology, Poland, in 1973 and 1979, respectively. He is a member of IEEE Computer Society, IFAC, and a chairman of IFIP Working Group 5.4 "Industrial Software Quality and Certification."

Notes